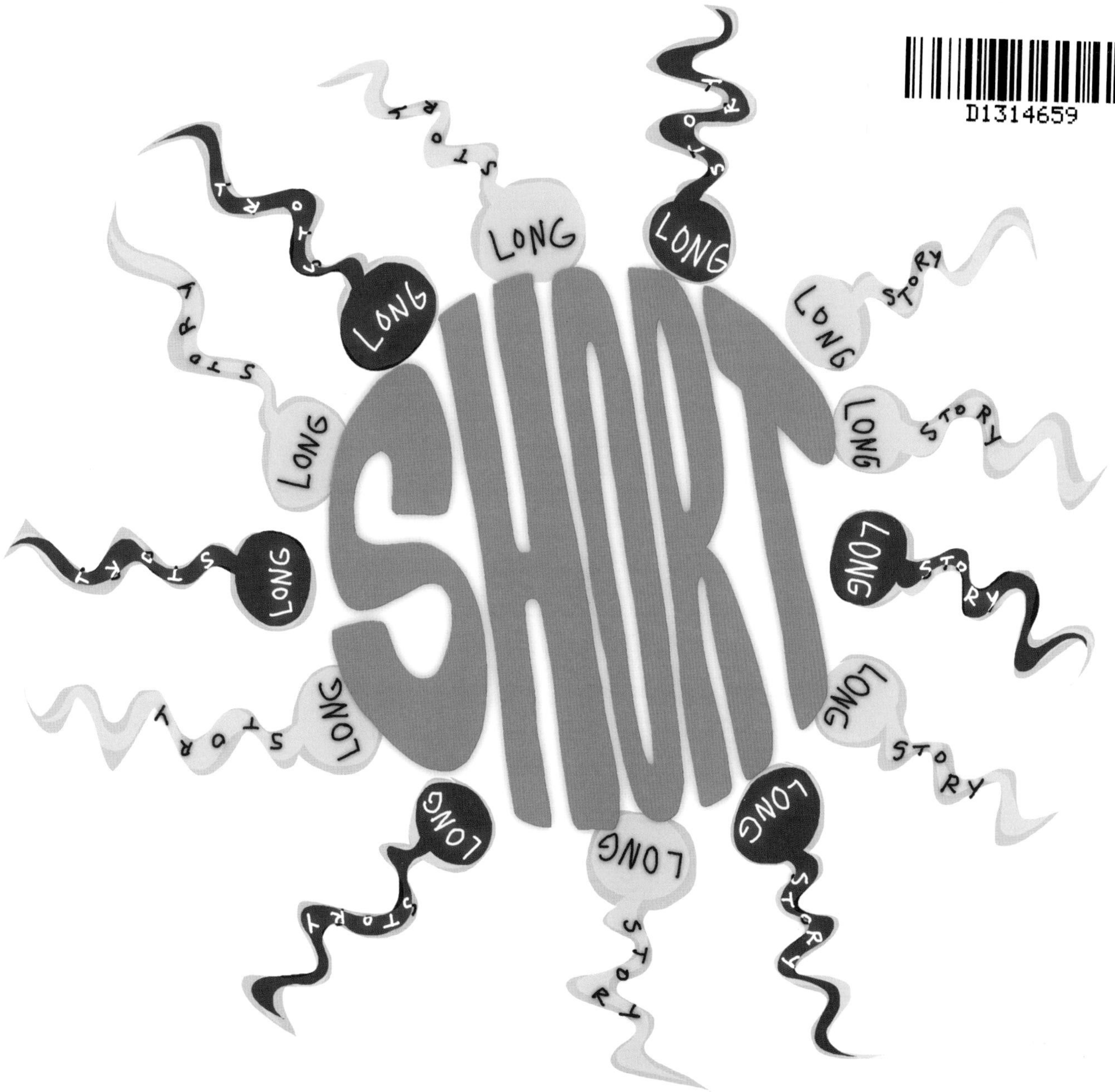
SHORT
LONG
STORY

All illustrations by Mr. Fish except where noted.

Published by Akashic Books
©2020 Mr. Fish

ISBN: 978-1-61775-796-9
Library of Congress Control Number: 2019943607
All rights reserved
First printing

Printed in Korea

Akashic Books
Brooklyn, New York, USA
Twitter: @AkashicBooks
Facebook: AkashicBooks
E-mail: info@akashicbooks.com
Website: www.akashicbooks.com

For Jack Benny,
who gave us all pause

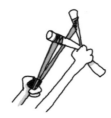

TABLE OF CONTENTS

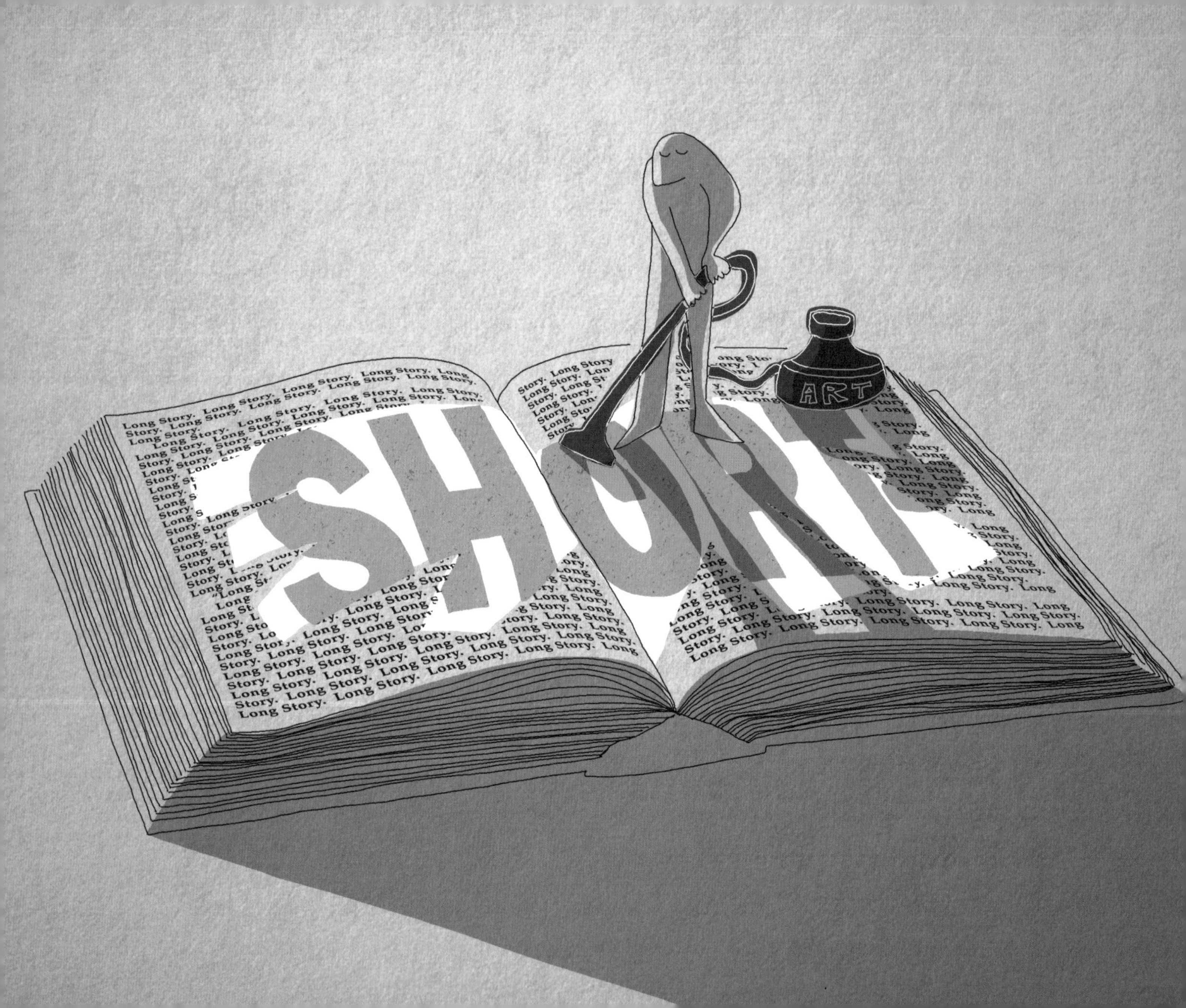
SHORT
ART
Long Story. Long Story. Long Story. Long Story.

INTRODUCTION

The book you now hold in your hand represents a collective effort by a disparate band of visual artists to use their expertise as painters, illustrators, graphic designers, and political cartoonists to capture the meaning and essence—perhaps even to reveal the deeper truths previously neglected by the keenest of readers—of some of the world's most famous books.

It is likely that you were told as a child by a grown-up who had finally had enough of your name-calling antics in the backyard or in the pool or in the living room or in the backseat of the car, or who saw your shrill refusal to try something new as an early-stage form of neofascism, that you cannot judge a book by its cover. This, of course, is not true.

How could it be? Had these adults never seen a copy of the magazines *Juggs* or *Black Inches*? Had they never considered the poison dart frogs of Central and South America, the monarch butterfly, or the Nerium oleander shrub, all of which had been rendered by evolution to be stilled explosions of the most dazzling and flamboyant colors found in nature for the express purpose of signaling profound toxicity to potential predators? These were books with covers that cued an absolute and urgent comprehension, the sort that relied on the most knee-jerk of judgments. In other words, hand somebody a book that has a photo on the cover of a 400-pound clown wearing an SS uniform who's crouching down and shoving a taxidermy squirrel that's holding an ashtray up his ass and the person is unlikely to read the title, *Antiquing with Greg,* and think, *Well, Nana's birthday is coming up and maybe there's something useful in here about Hummels and Depression glass.*

The fact is, an image, whether snapped or rendered, does something that the written word cannot: it communicates a version of reality instantaneously, one that informs immediately without first needing to be assembled brick by syntactic brick, then cognitively deciphered and then paired with the appropriate sense memory, moral contrivance, and rote definition before its meaning and intentions can be made clear. After all, words and ideas are conceptual and do not present themselves to our senses where real-life objects do, meaning that to engage with a visual representation of a person, place, or thing is likely the most accurate way in which to capture, communicate, and, therefore, commune with existence, short of engaging with it directly, with hands, lips, flaring nostrils, and pressing flesh. The Sumerians didn't invent the written word until 3500 BCE, meaning that for nearly 37,000 years before that, according to the evidentiary record regarding cave art and prehistoric sculptures and carvings, an entirely illiterate humanity relied on an image-based language for the logging of its history, the articulation of its passions, and the grounding of its spiritual collaboration with the mystical, suggesting perhaps that the invention of words might've been less a product of necessity and more an expression of superfluous curiosity, like the invention of carbonated water or the Internet or Velcro.

A literal depiction shares the self-defining expediency communicated by life itself and, unlike its lingual counterpart, is automatic, the difference between reading the word *sunset* or *shit* or *sinew* and coming face-to-face with a depiction of any one of those things; *things* that illiteracy cannot confound and only the subterfuge of symbolism can camouflage. In that way, an image is not merely an idea *about* truth, but rather its direct reflection and its closest approximation—specifically, words represent how we communicate with reality, while images represent how reality communicates with us.

Of course, a language that reflects the primary element of reality directly will always be a more credible source for accuracy over a lexiconic translation based on apocryphal concepts of reality, which is why cartoonists, for hundreds of years, when not crafting frivolous graphic confectionery for greeting card companies, advertising conglomerates, and corporate circulars, have been skilled interpreters of cacophonous bombast, usually of the political variety, and keen decoders of the various cultural contrivances that bombard and oftentimes perplex us every day. By condensing complex accounts of either truth or beauty into serviceable visual encapsulations, a cartoonist brings agility to the public's thinking, comprehension to dissonance, and clarity to any number of confounding questions by providing nonverbal proofs as part of the deductive reasoning process. A cartoonist, whether an unapologetic slasher and burner of political balderdash, a pyrotechnic igniter of enlightening insights, or a propagator of something as beautiful and mandatory as genuine and unifying laughter, only succeeds when he or she is concise and lean and succinct while exercising his or her craft in deference to the explicit probity of reality itself, the idea being that when presenting a counterfeit facsimile of a base vérité—one that hopes to curb and possibly even eliminate the perpetuation of loquacious and distracting bullshit, which, by the way, is completely man-made and does not exist in nature— simplicity is key.

Long Story Short is a book that both demonstrates and celebrates the visual artist's ability to boil down complicated narratives into more precise aggregates. What follows is a collection of drawings and paintings rendered by many of the country's leading cartoonists and illustrators to reveal the theme and function of some of the most popular and significant books ever written. How? By eliminating the writing, of course—or at least minimizing it. Each contribution is an attempt to look past the printed page as if it were sheet music and to find the music—and then to play it.

MR.FISH

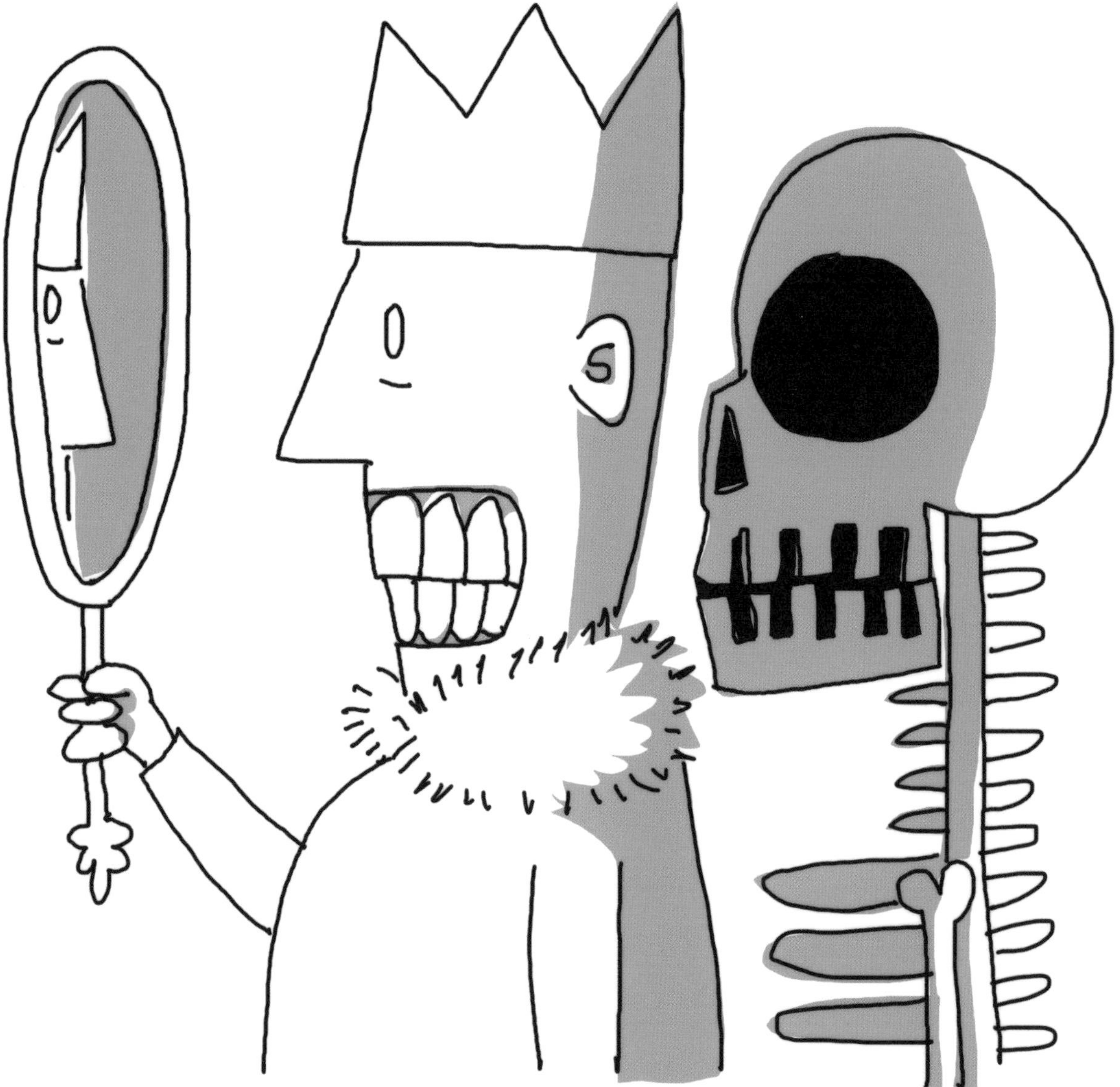

THE CATCHER IN THE RYE

J. D. Salinger

ILLUSTRATION BY TAMARA KNOSS

"Goddam money. It always ends up making you blue as hell."

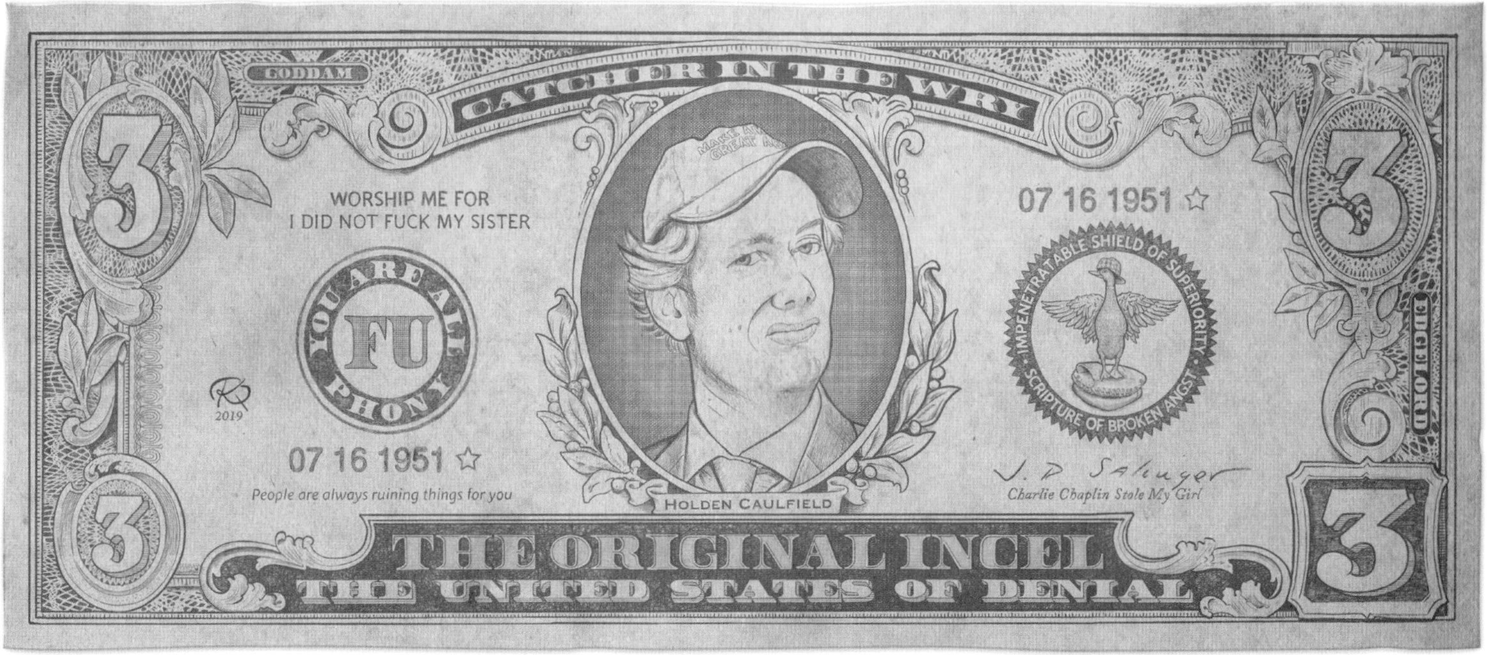
GODDAM
CATCHER IN THE WRY
WORSHIP ME FOR
I DID NOT FUCK MY SISTER
07 16 1951 ☆
YOU ARE ALL PHONY
FU
2019
07 16 1951 ☆
People are always ruining things for you
HOLDEN CAULFIELD
IMPENETRATABLE SHIELD OF SUPERIORITY
SCRIPTURE OF BROKEN ANGST
J. D. Salinger
Charlie Chaplin Stole My Girl
THE ORIGINAL INCEL
THE UNITED STATES OF DENIAL
3

LOLITA

Vladimir Nabokov

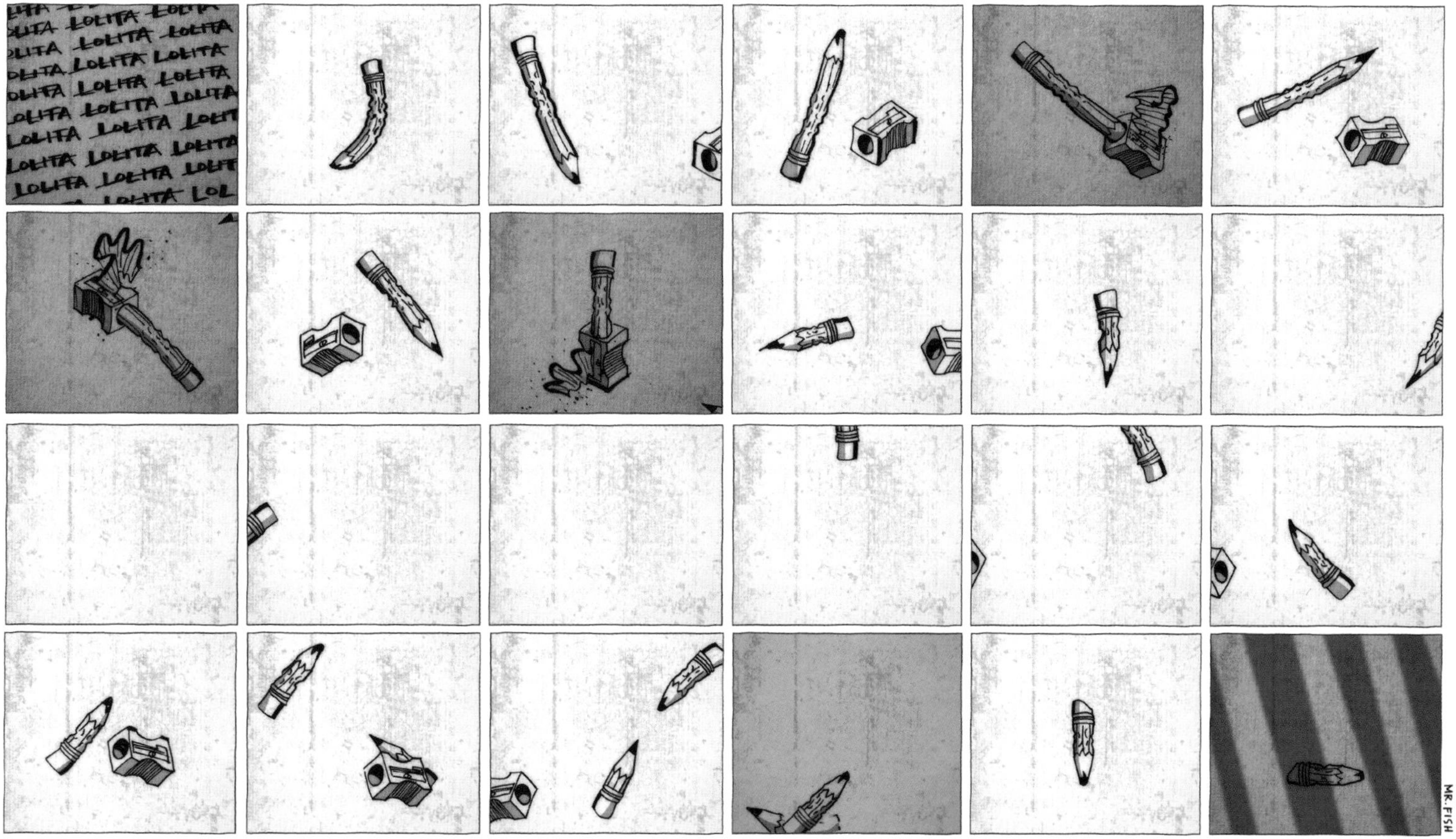
LOLITA LOLITA
LOLITA LOLITA
LOLITA LOLITA
LOLITA LOLITA
LOLITA LOLITA
LOLITA LOLITA
LOLITA LOLITA
LOLITA
MR. FISH

NATIVE SON
Richard Wright

ILLUSTRATION BY KEITH HENRY BROWN

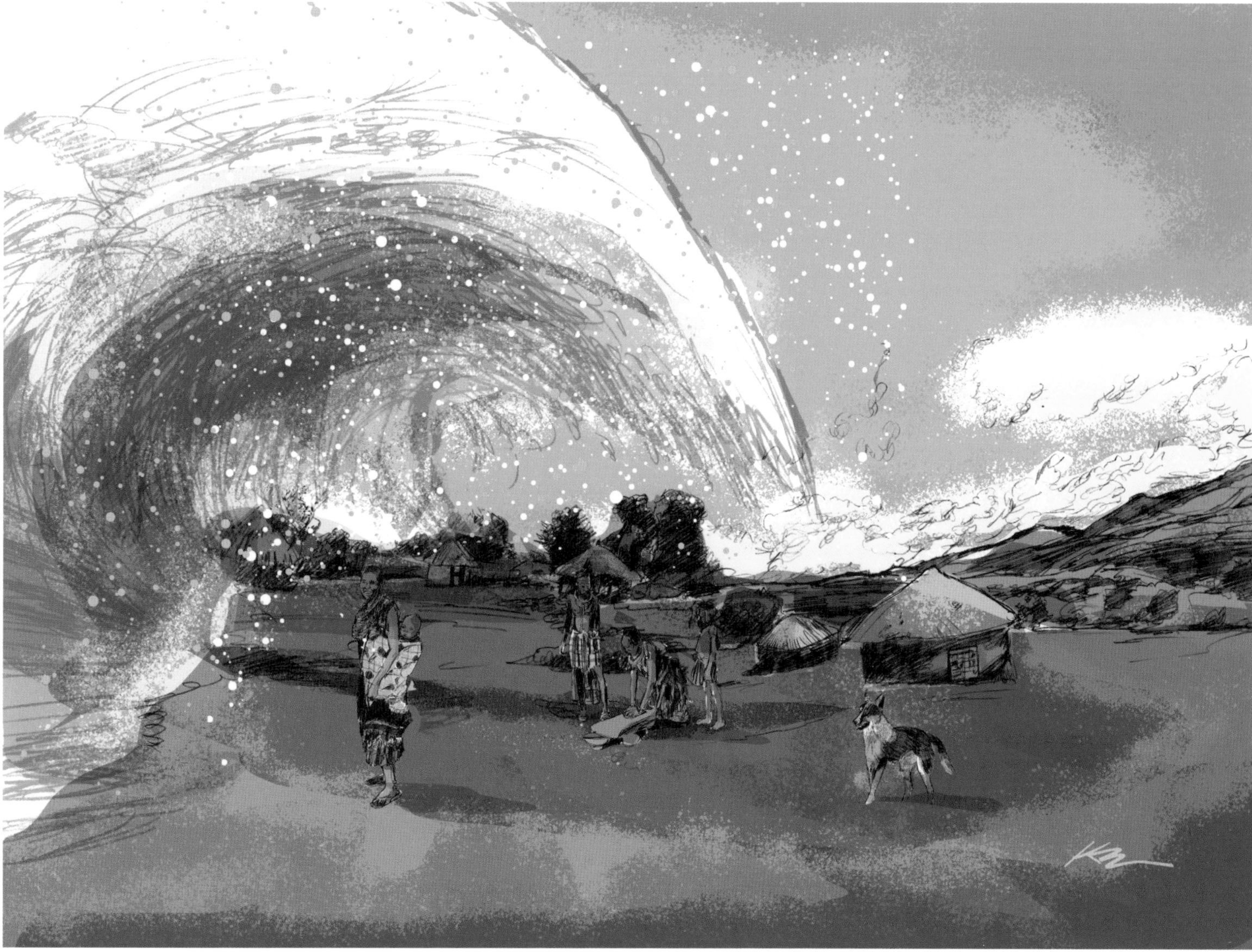

FRANKENSTEIN
Mary Shelley

ILLUSTRATION BY ELI VALLEY

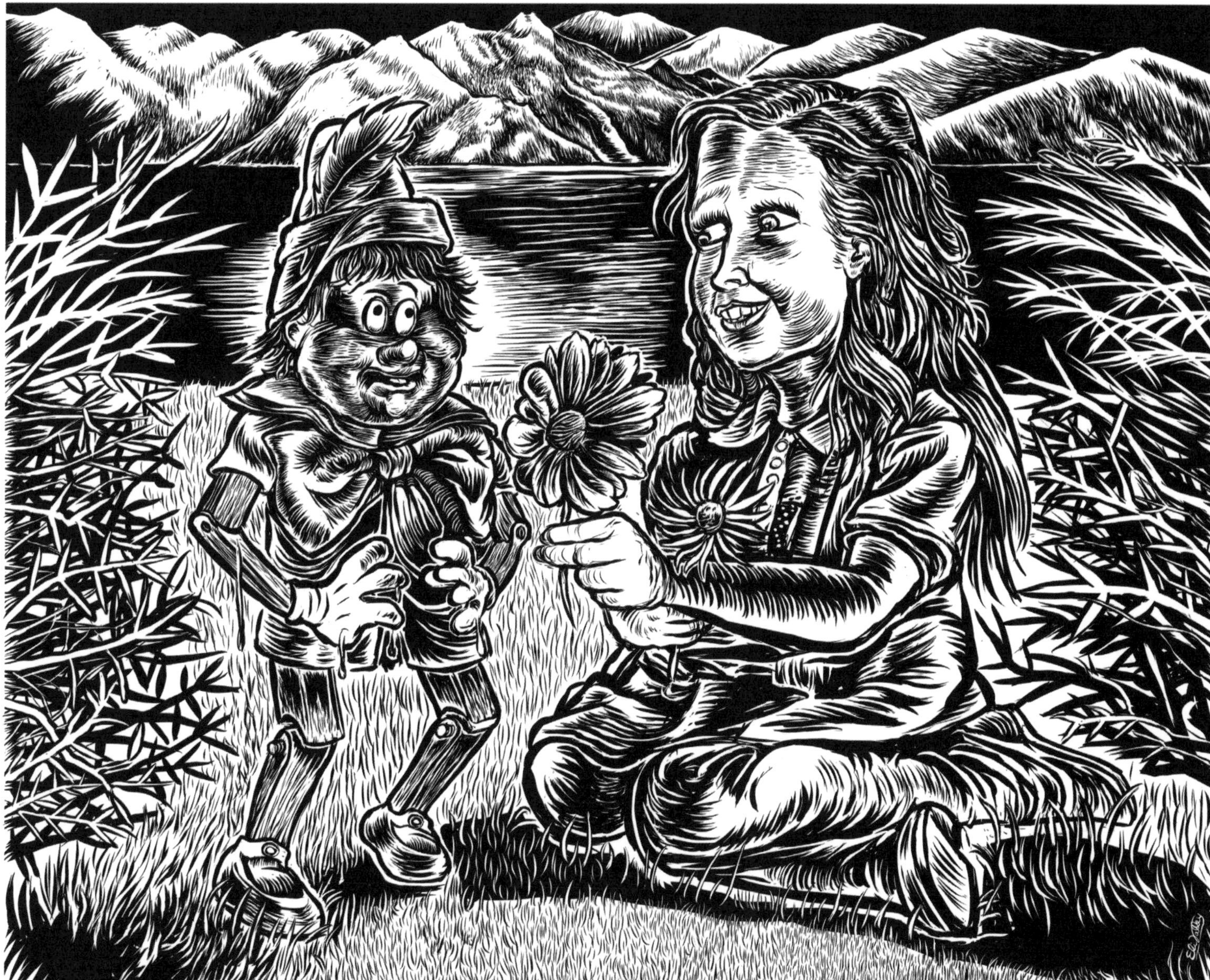

THE ELECTRIC KOOL-AID ACID TEST

Tom Wolfe

ILLUSTRATION BY WES TYRELL

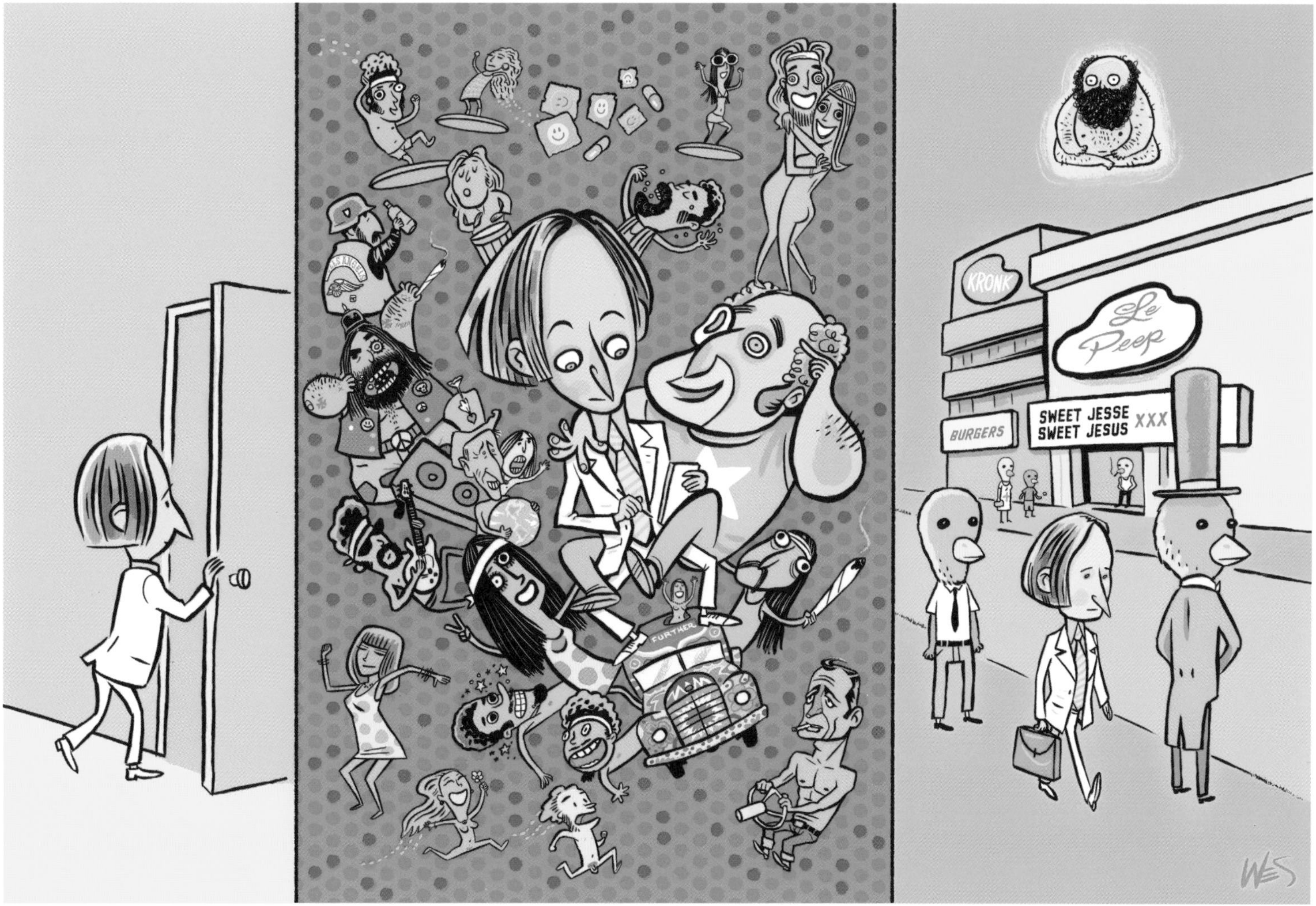
KRONK
Le Peep
SWEET JESSE
SWEET JESUS
XXX
BURGERS
FURTHER
WES

THE NEW TESTAMENT

Paul the Apostle

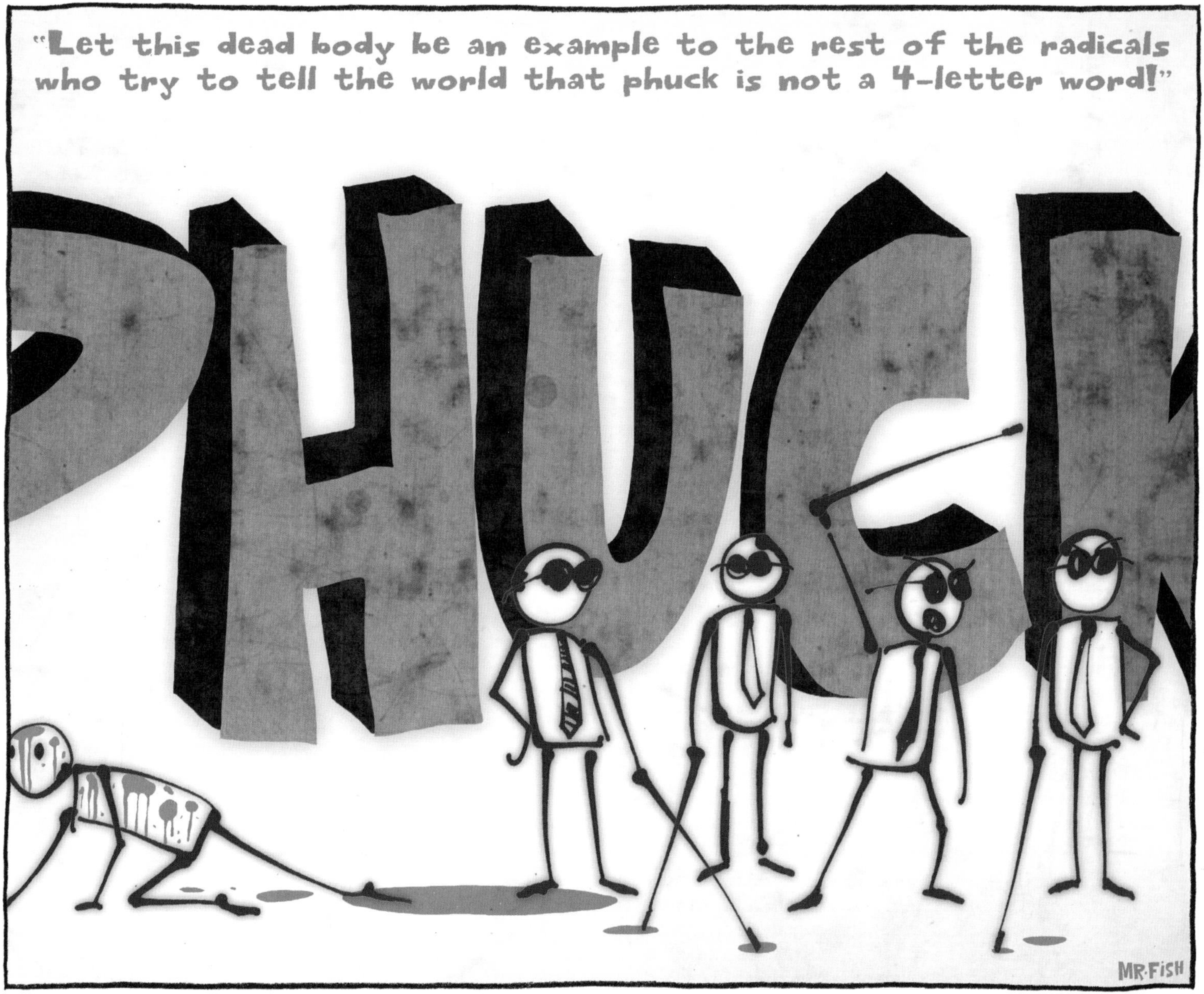
"Let this dead body be an example to the rest of the radicals who try to tell the world that phuck is not a 4-letter word!"
PHUCK
MR. FISH

SLAUGHTERHOUSE-FIVE
Kurt Vonnegut

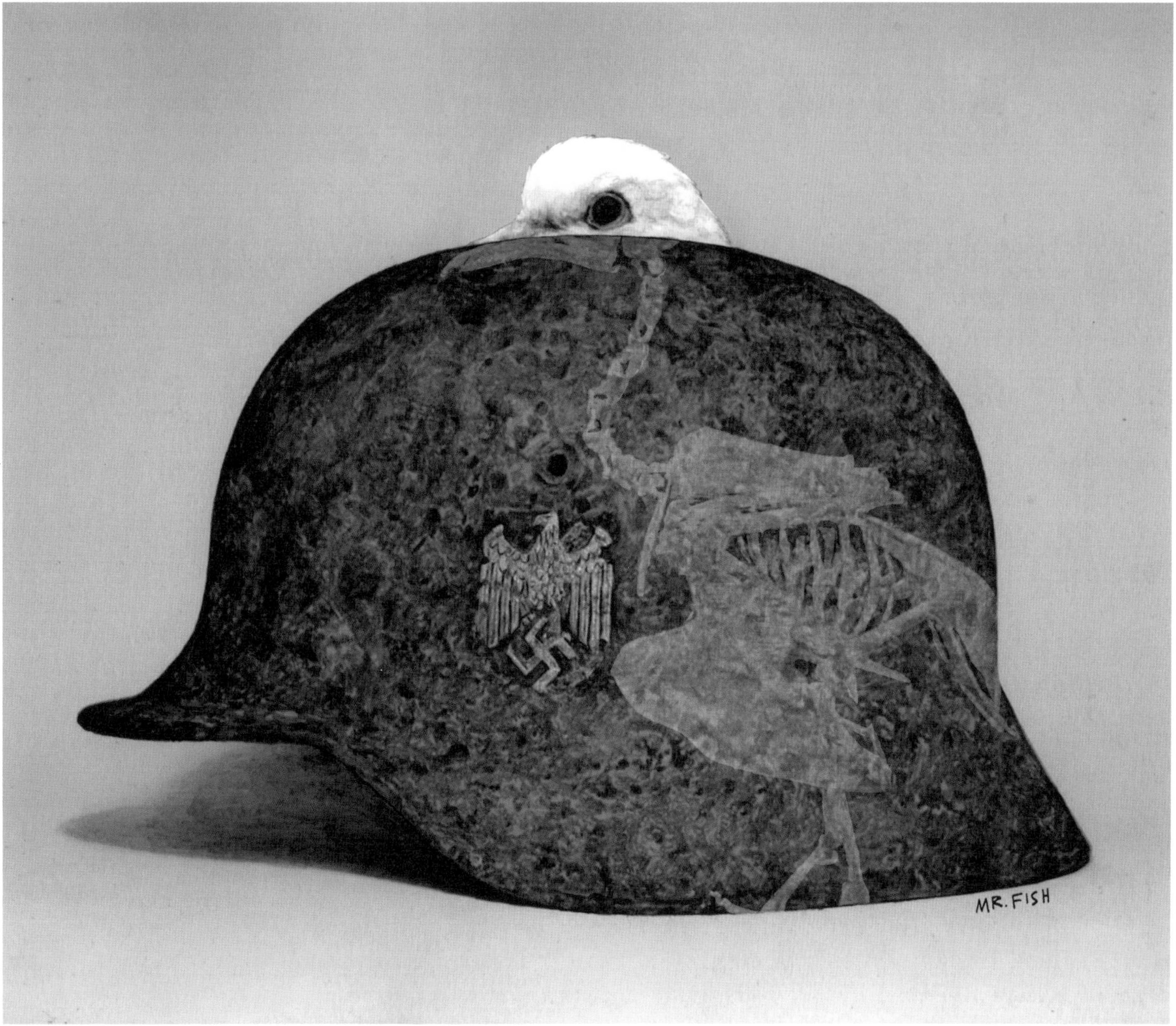
MR. FISH

MOBY-DICK

Herman Melville

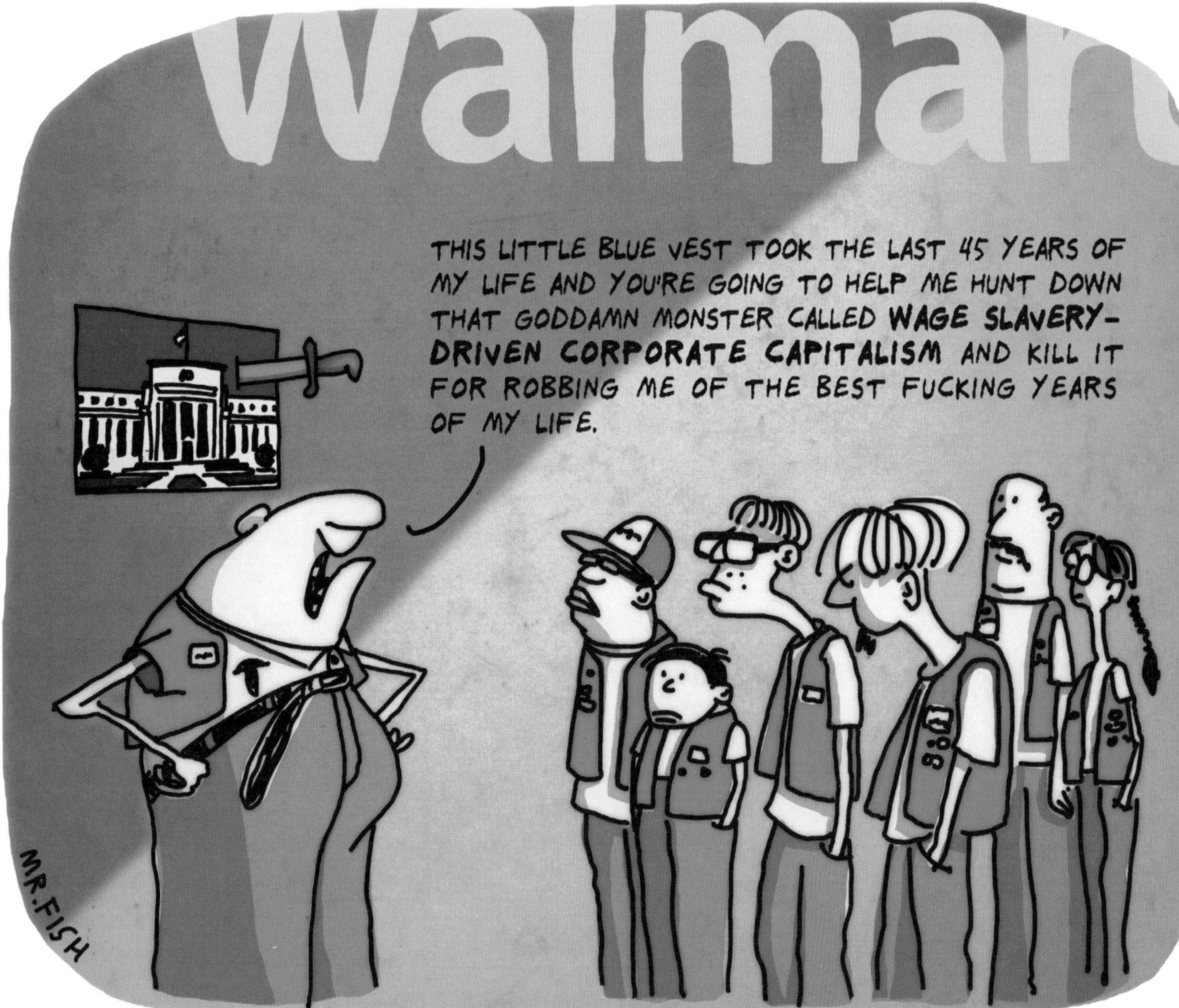
walmar
THIS LITTLE BLUE VEST TOOK THE LAST 45 YEARS OF MY LIFE AND YOU'RE GOING TO HELP ME HUNT DOWN THAT GODDAMN MONSTER CALLED WAGE SLAVERY-DRIVEN CORPORATE CAPITALISM AND KILL IT FOR ROBBING ME OF THE BEST FUCKING YEARS OF MY LIFE.
MR.FISH

THE RINGS OF SATURN

W. G. Sebald

ILLUSTRATION BY SARAH AWAD

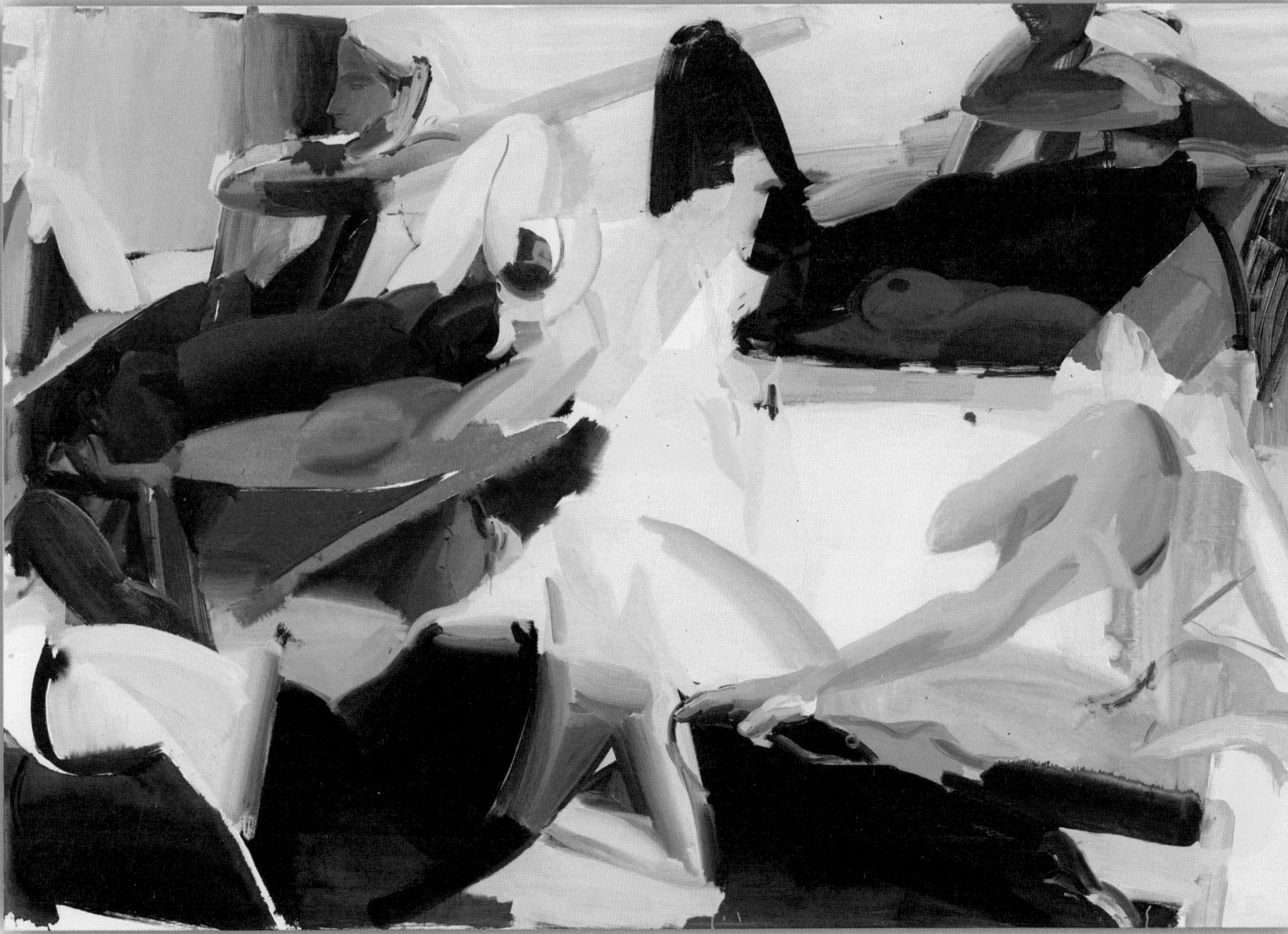

"The disturbing thing about mirrors, and also the act of copulation, is that they multiply the number of human beings."
—*Jorge Luis Borges, from* Tlön, Uqbar, Orbis Tertius

HAMLET

William Shakespeare

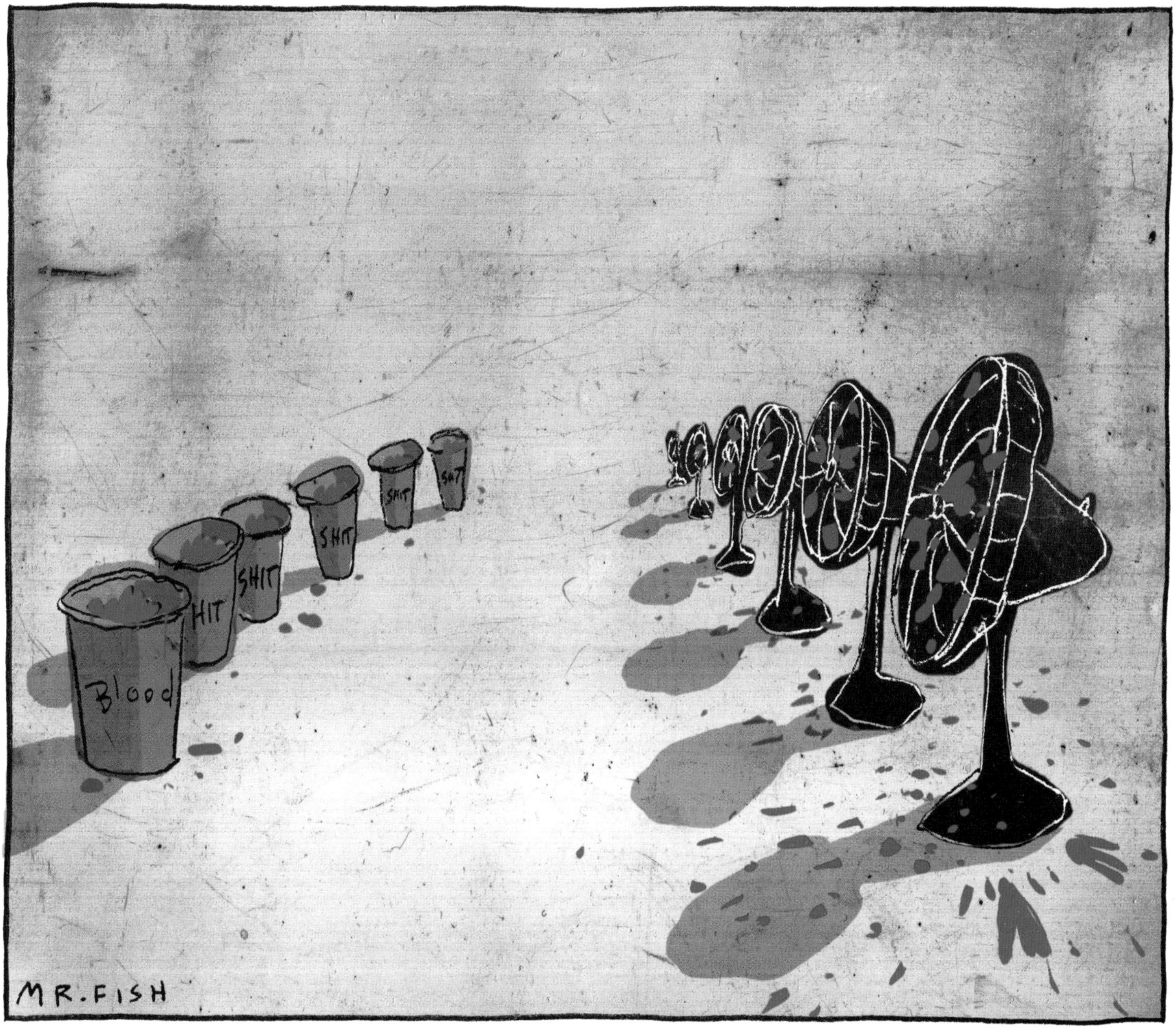
Blood
HIT
SHIT
SHIT
SHIT
SHIT
MR. FISH

THE PICTURE OF DORIAN GRAY

Oscar Wilde

ILLUSTRATION BY SAM HENDERSON

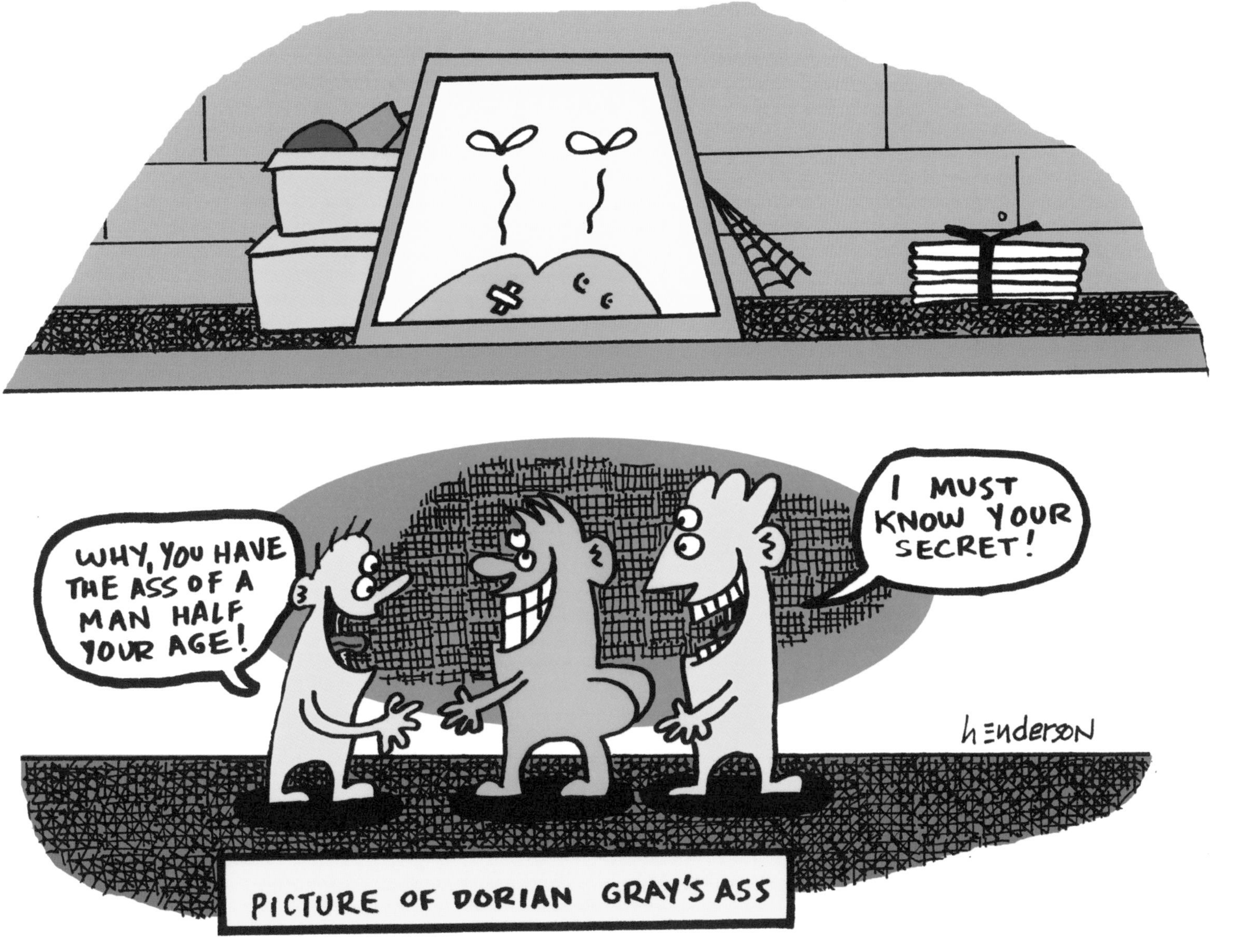
WHY, YOU HAVE THE ASS OF A MAN HALF YOUR AGE!
I MUST KNOW YOUR SECRET!
henderson
PICTURE OF DORIAN GRAY'S ASS

THE METAMORPHOSIS

Franz Kafka

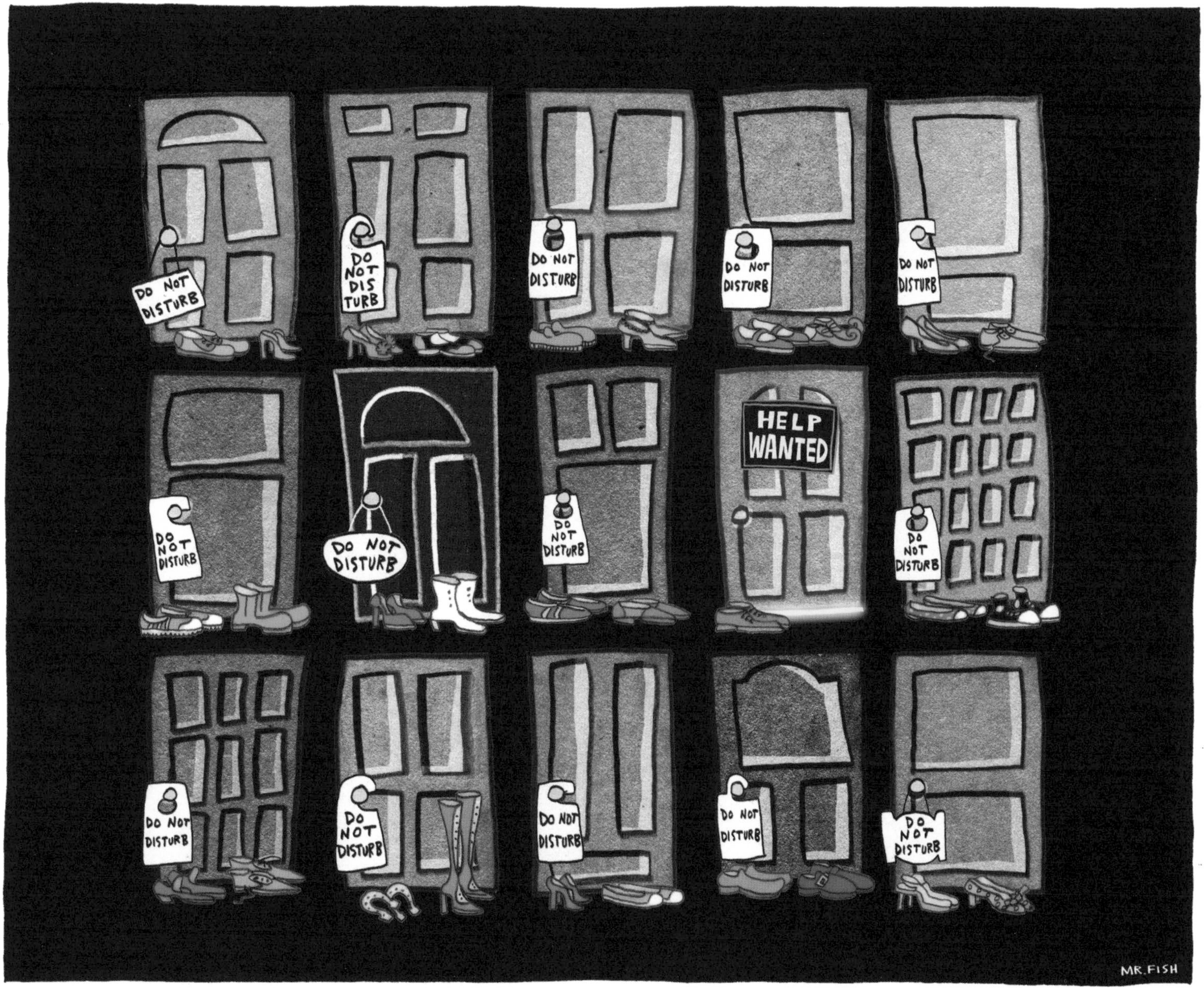
DO NOT DISTURB
DO NOT DIS TURB
DO NOT DISTURB
DO NOT DISTURB
DO NOT DISTURB
DO NOT DISTURB
DO NOT DISTURB
DO NOT DISTURB
HELP WANTED
DO NOT DISTURB
DO NOT DISTURB
DO NOT DISTURB
DO NOT DISTURB
DO NOT DISTURB
DO NOT DISTURB
MR. FISH

THE SCARLET LETTER

Nathaniel Hawthorne

ILLUSTRATION BY TED RALL

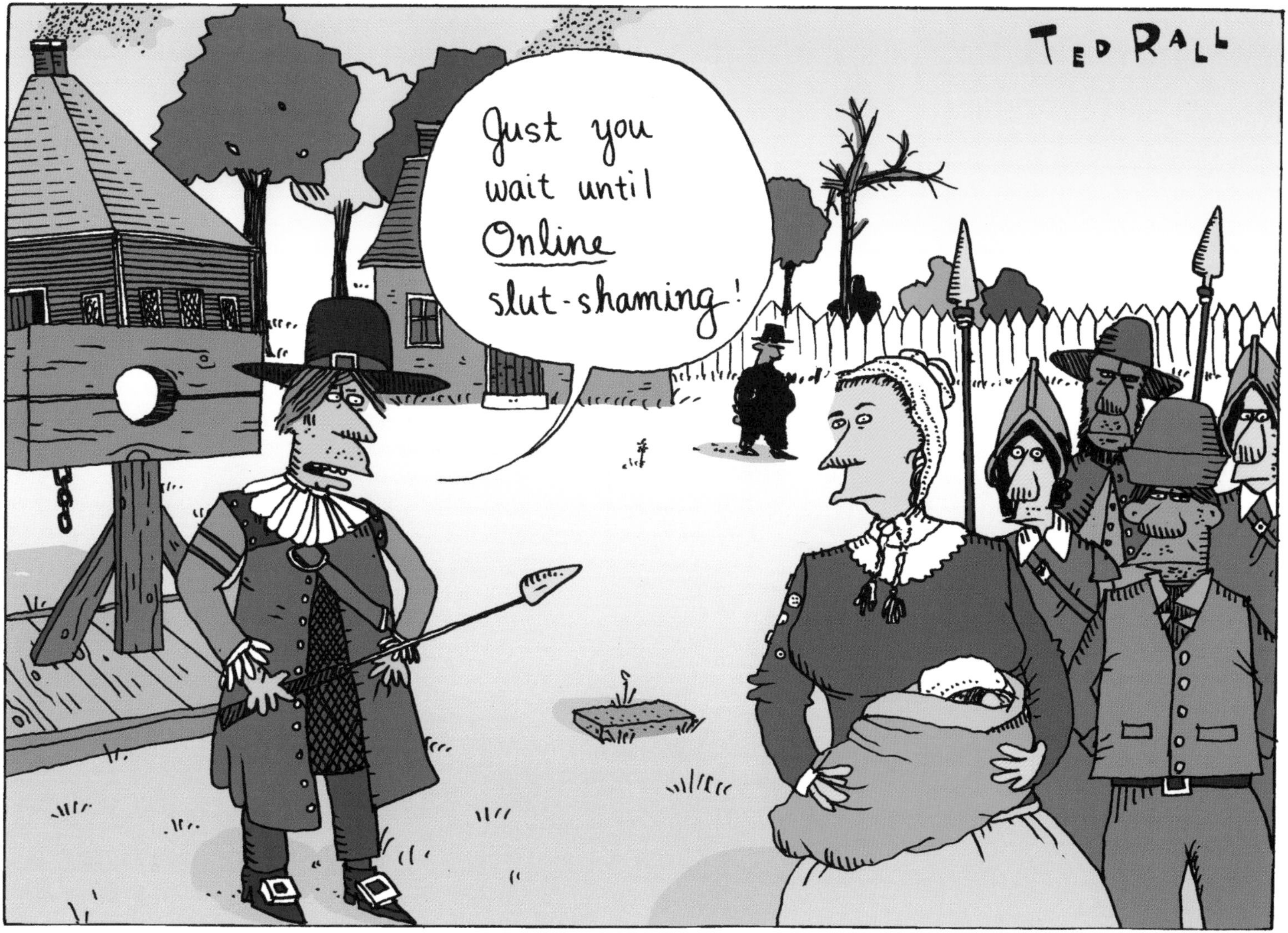
TED RALL
Just you wait until Online slut-shaming!

ROGET'S THESAURUS

Peter Mark Roget

ILLUSTRATION BY LODI MARASESCU

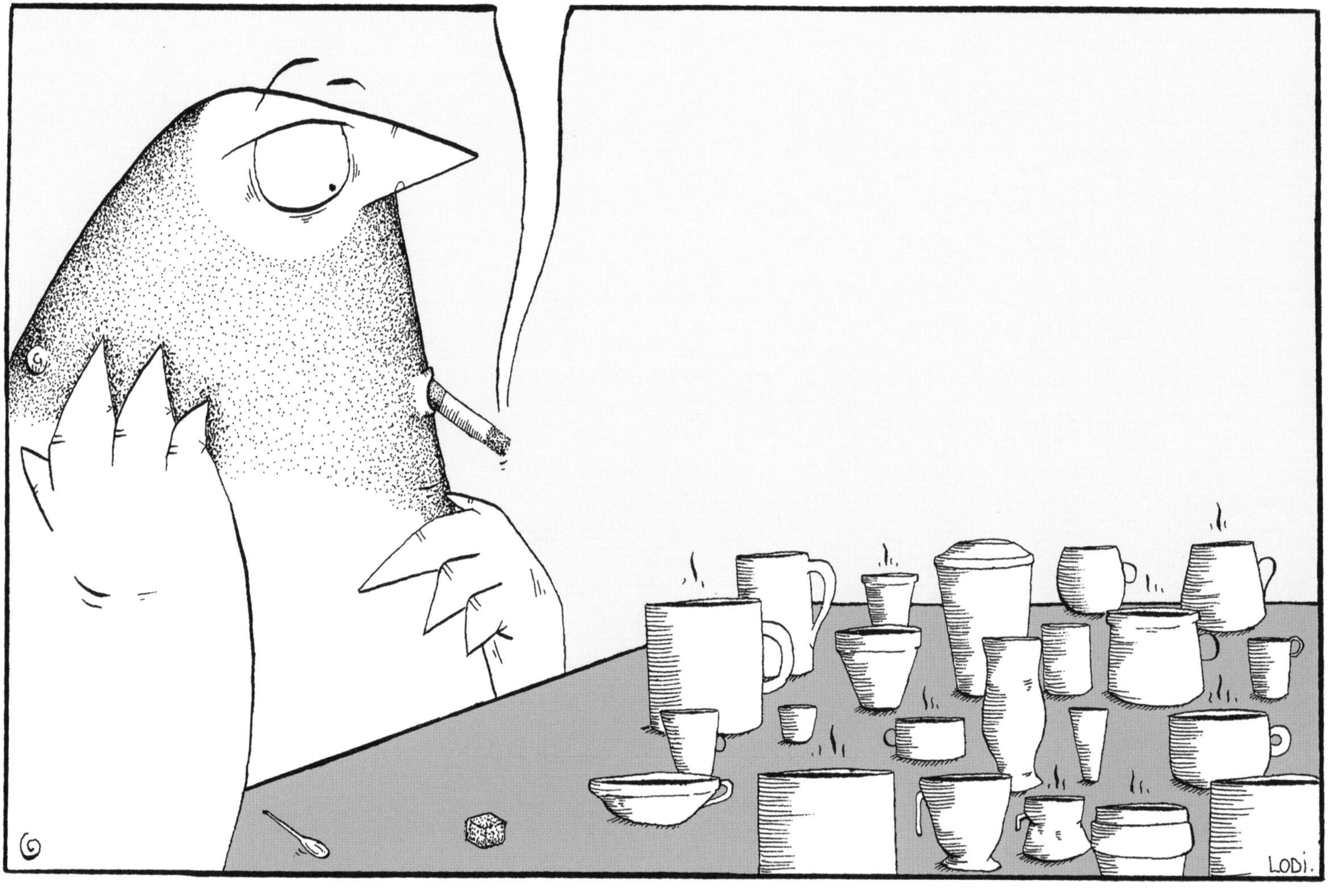
LODI.

CHARLIE AND THE CHOCOLATE FACTORY
Roald Dahl

ILLUSTRATION BY SURAG RAMACHANDRAN

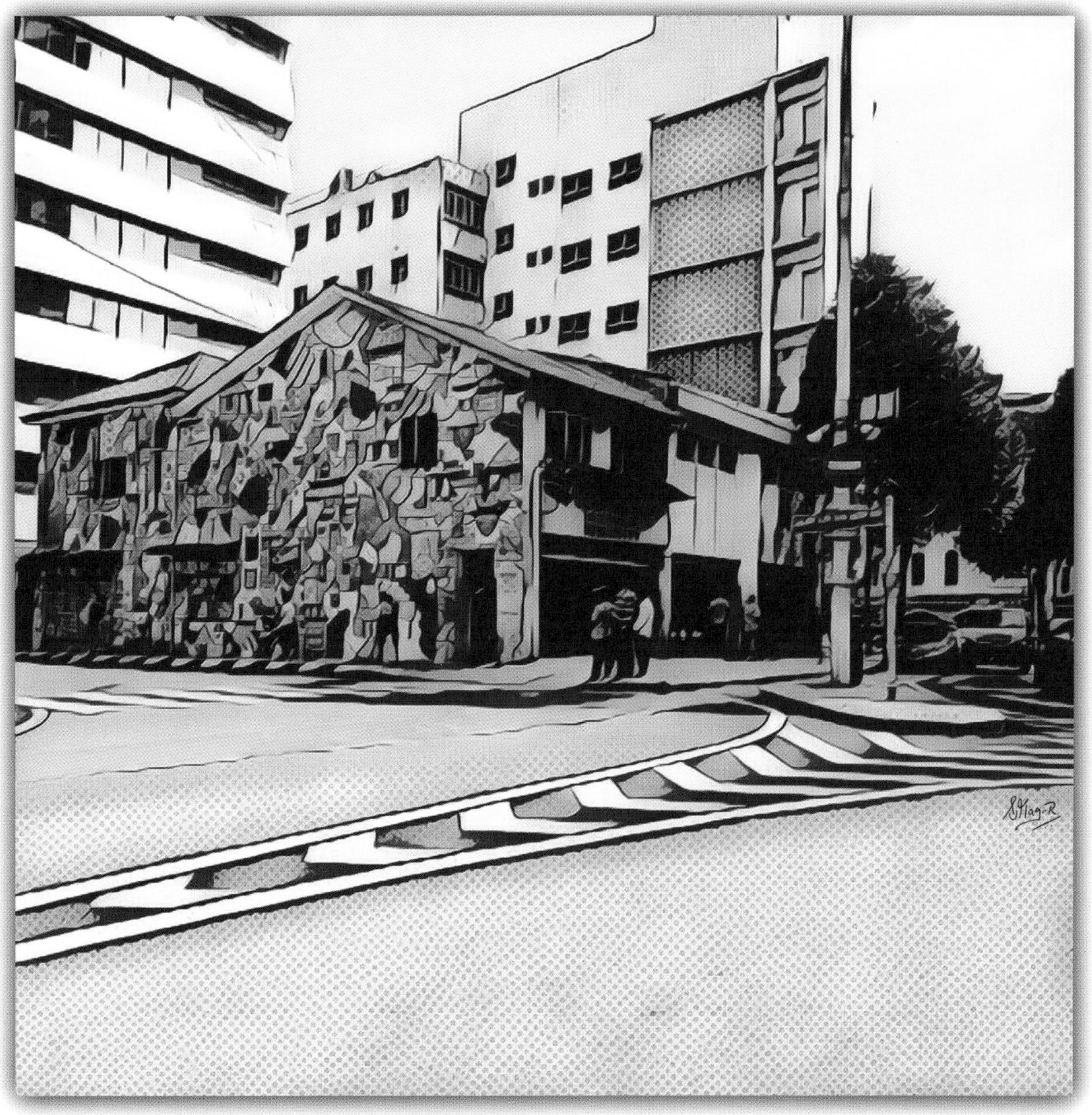

MADAME BOVARY

Gustave Flaubert

Time was running out for Sperm Bank to find true love.

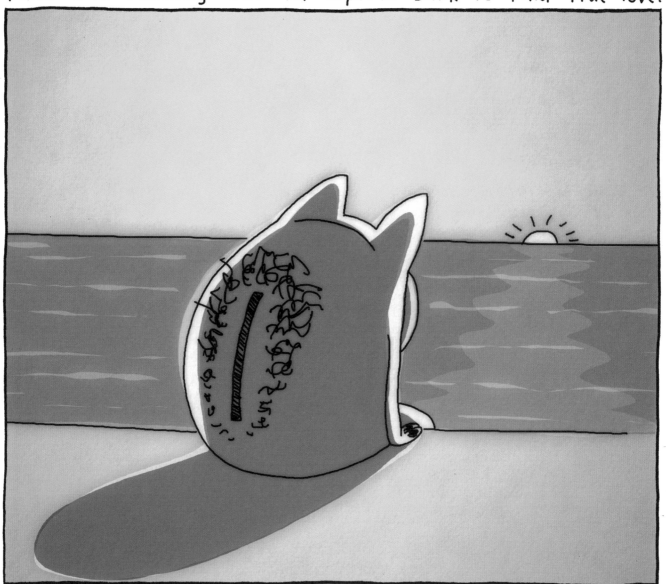

MR·FISH

THE COMMUNIST MANIFESTO

Karl Marx and Friedrich Engels

ILLUSTRATION BY STEPHANIE McMILLAN

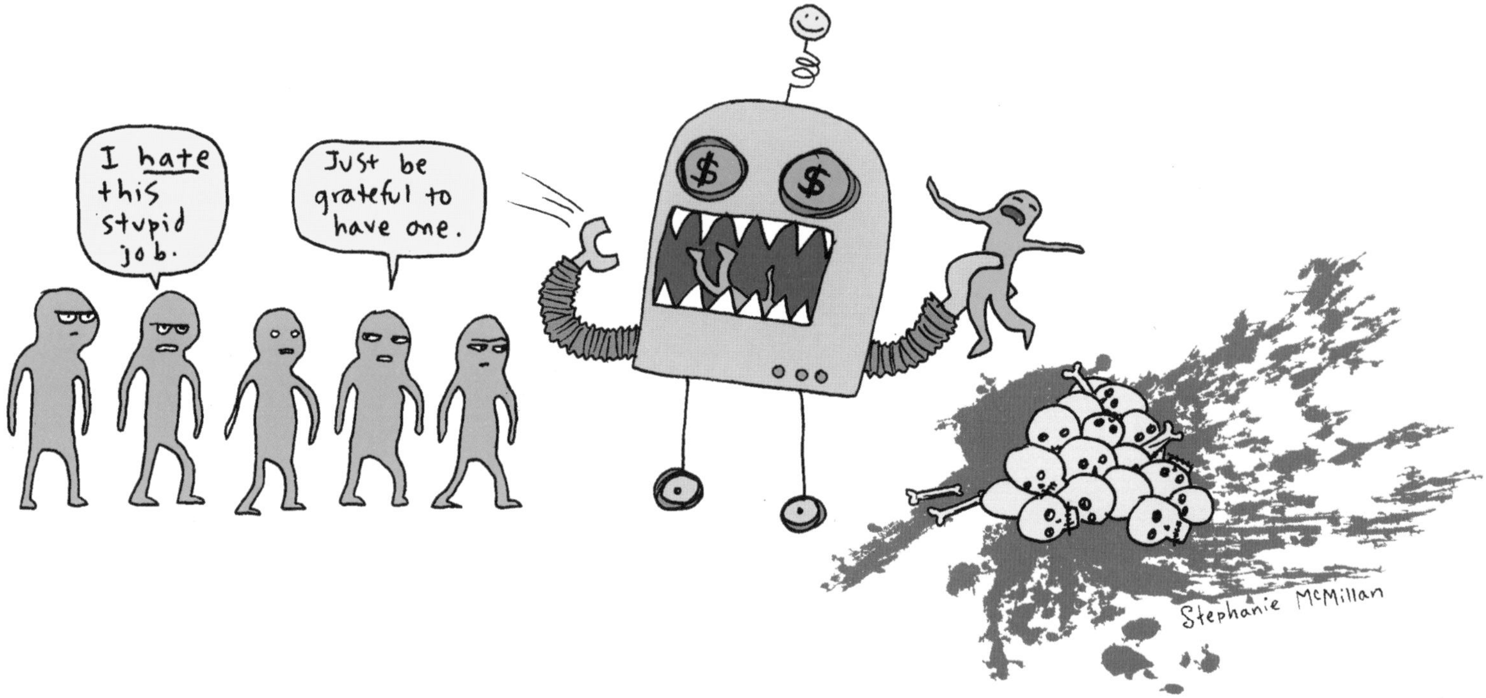
I hate this stupid job.
Just be grateful to have one.
Stephanie McMillan

OZYMANDIAS

Percy Bysshe Shelley and Horace Smith

ILLUSTRATION BY TAMI KNIGHT

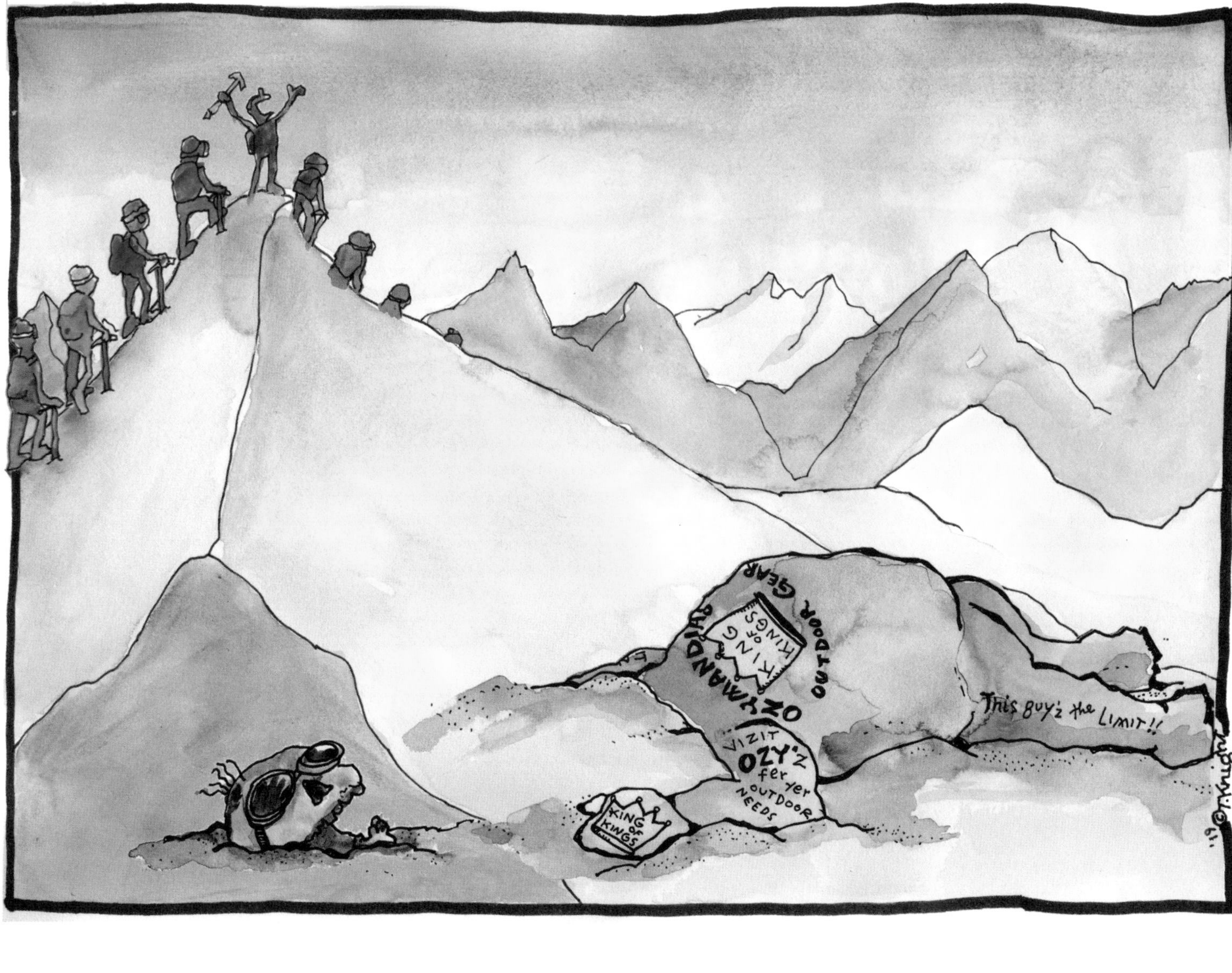
OZYMANDIAS OUTDOOR GEAR
KING OF KINGS
This Guy'z the LIMIT!!
VIZIT OZY'Z fer yer OUTDOOR NEEDS
KING OF KINGS
©T.Knight '19

HOW TO WIN FRIENDS AND INFLUENCE PEOPLE

Dale Carnegie

MR. FISH

I AM JOAQUÍN / YO SOY JOAQUÍN

Rodolfo "Corky" Gonzales

ILLUSTRATION BY ERIC J. GARCIA

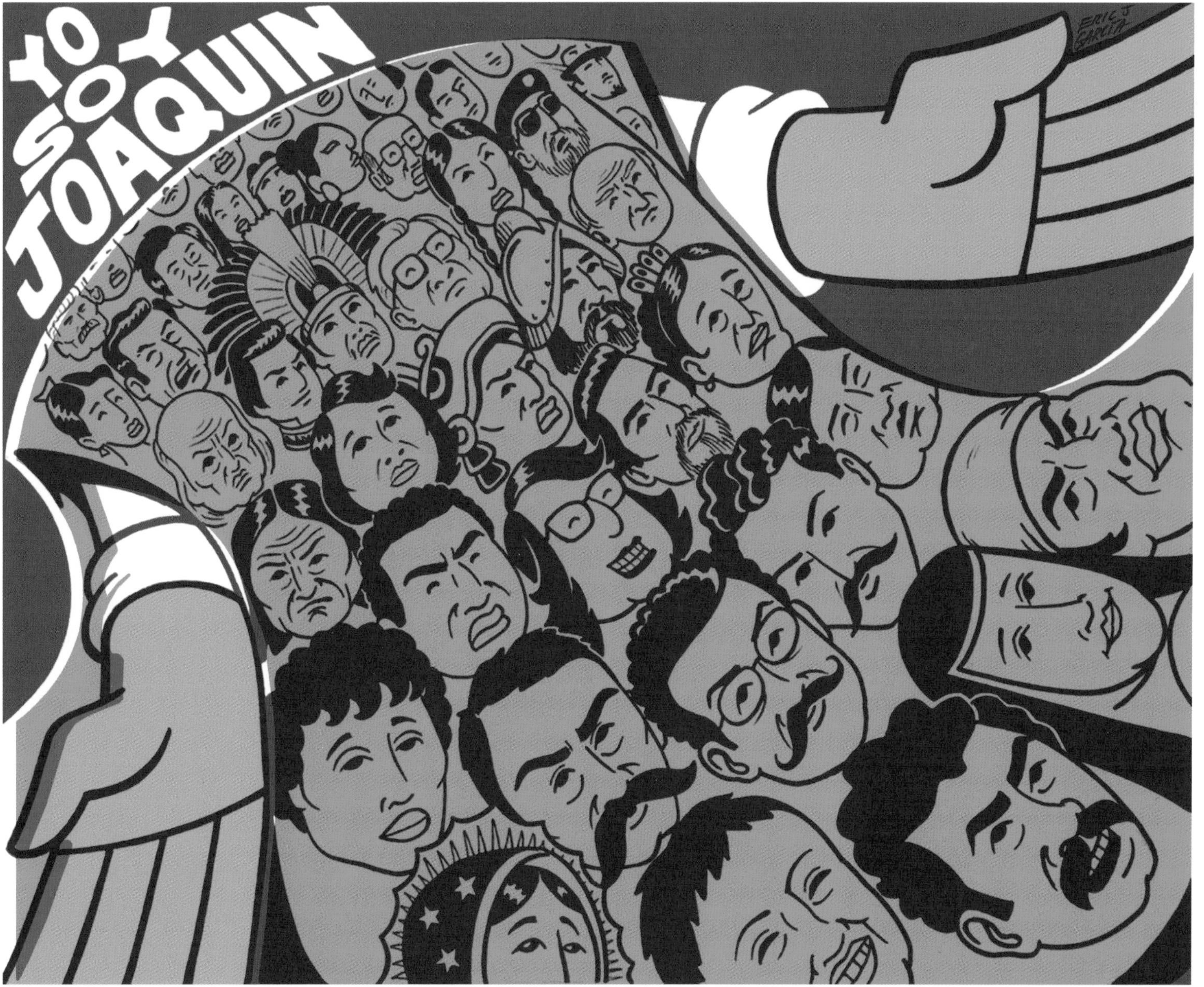
YO SOY JOAQUIN
ERIC J GARCIA

THE ANARCHIST COOKBOOK

William Powell

ILLUSTRATION BY MARISSA DOUGHERTY

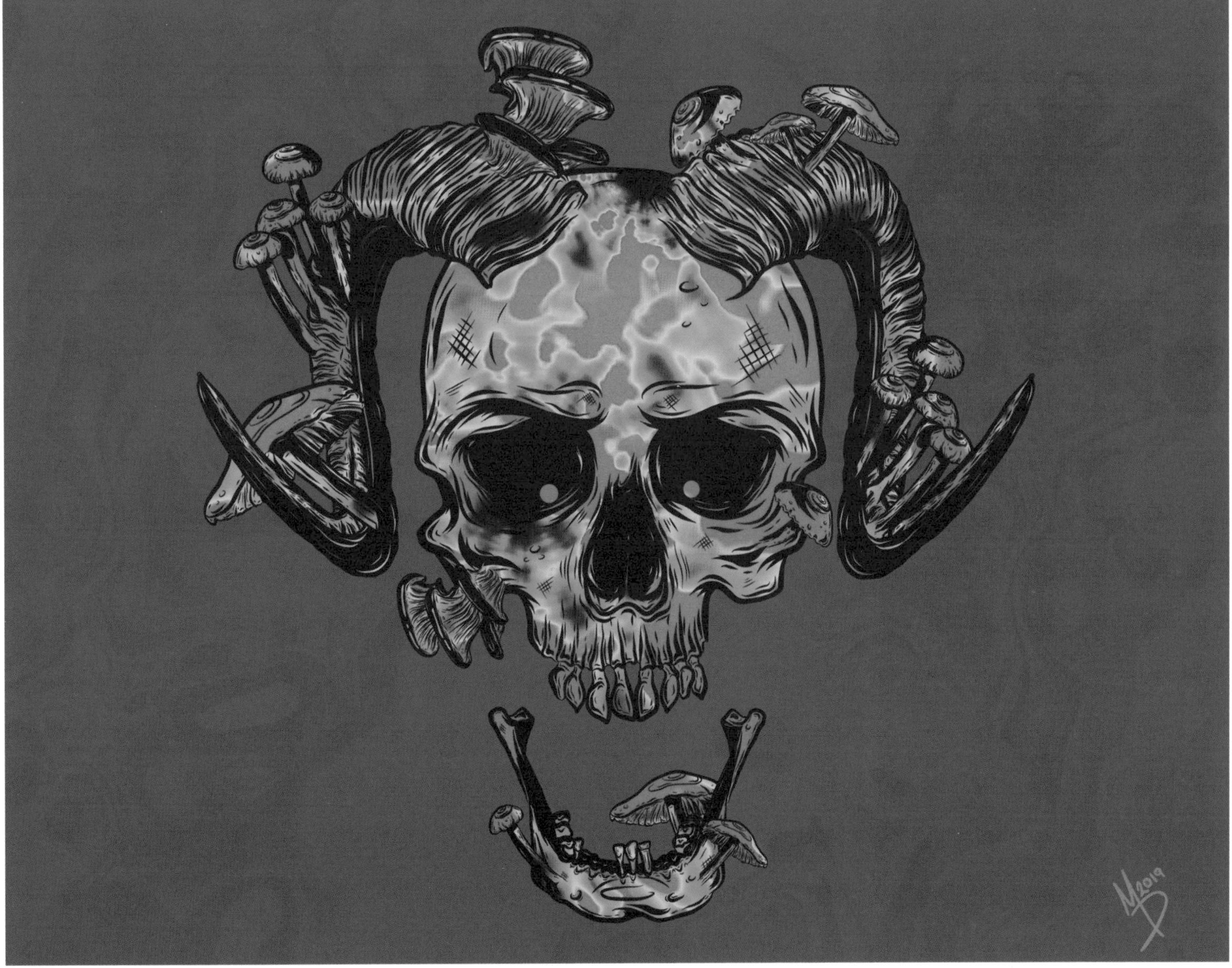

A BRIEF HISTORY OF TIME
Stephen Hawking

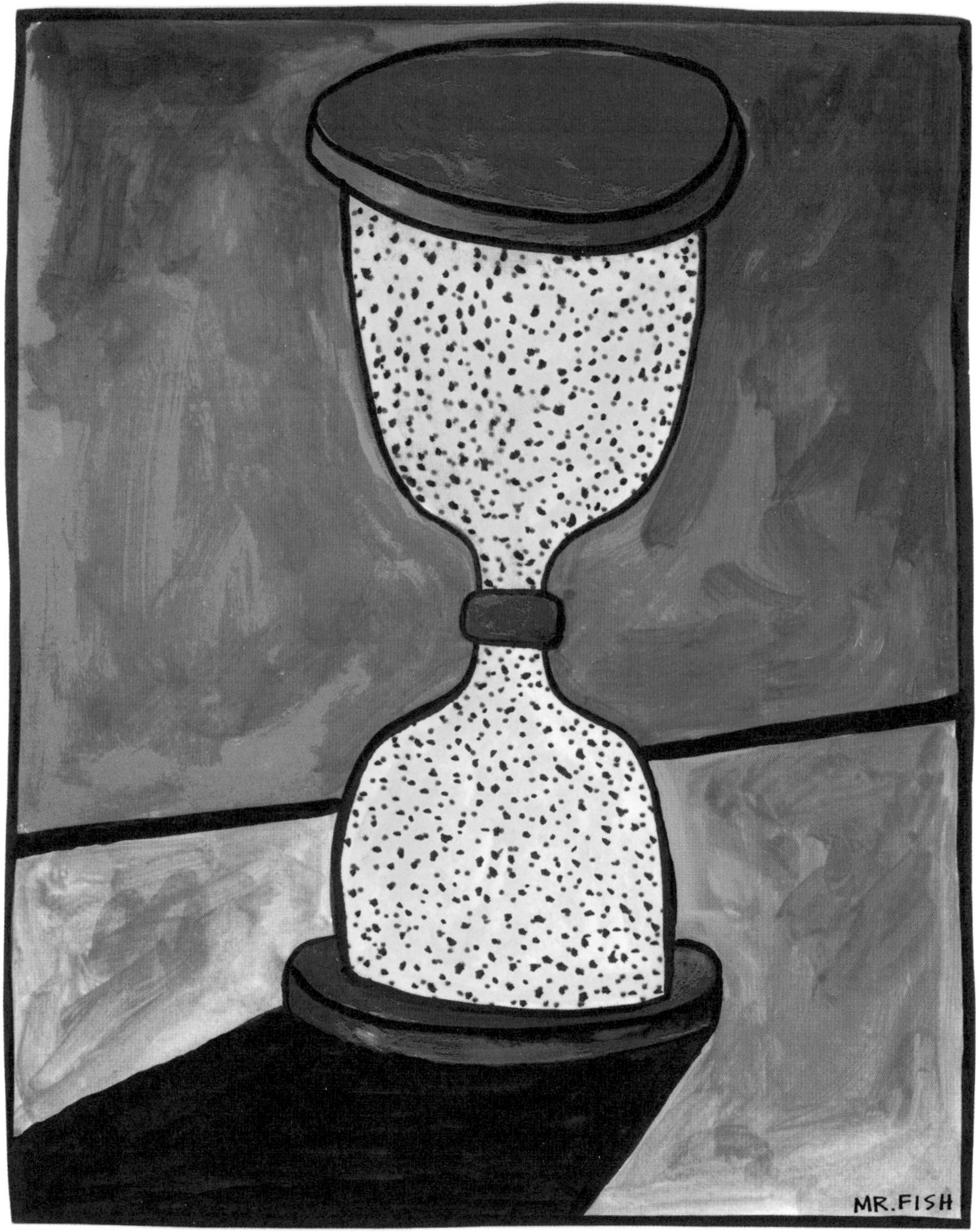
MR.FISH

BRAVE NEW WORLD

Aldous Huxley

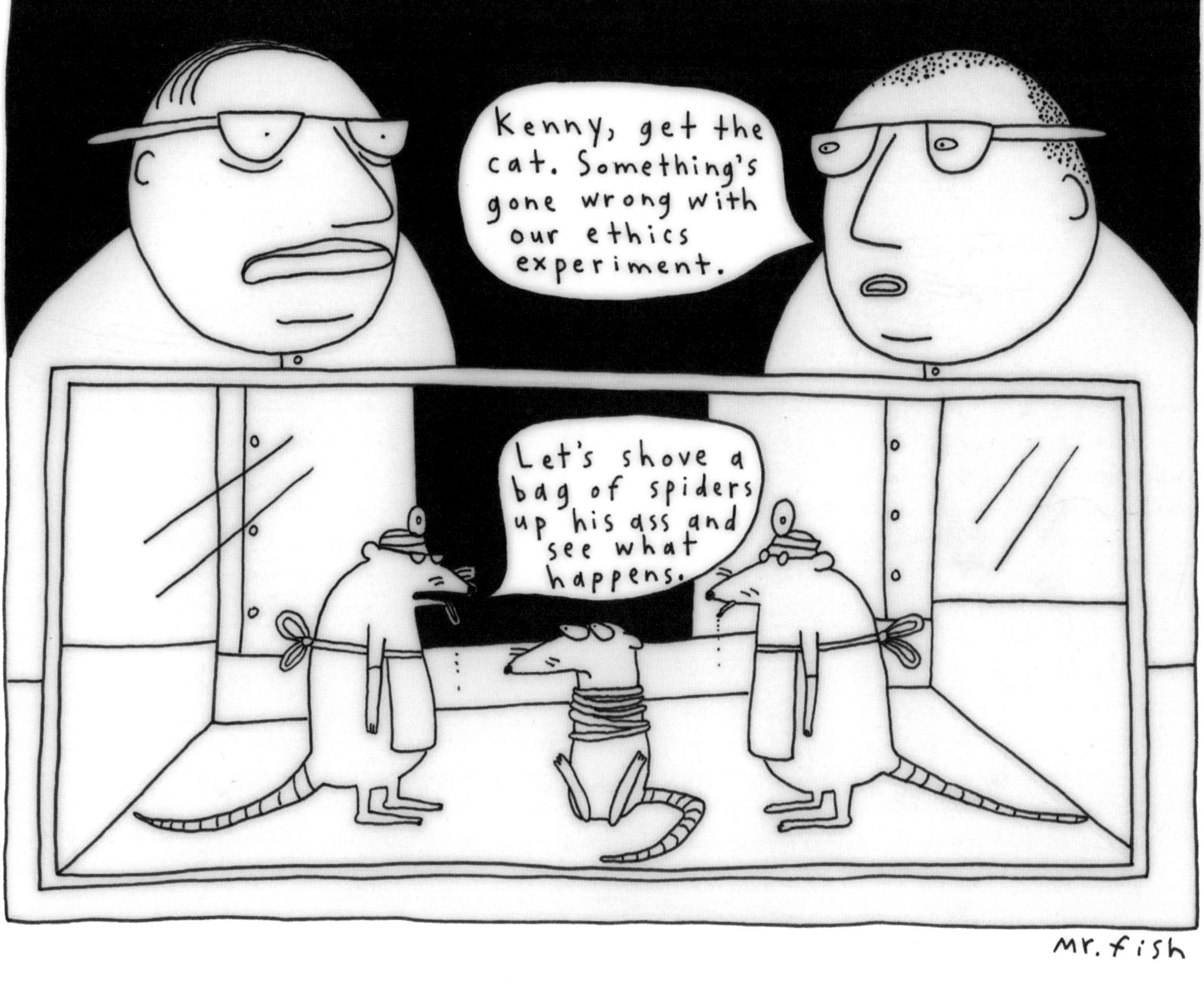
Kenny, get the cat. Something's gone wrong with our ethics experiment.
Let's shove a bag of spiders up his ass and see what happens.
MR. FISH

ADVENTURES OF HUCKLEBERRY FINN

Mark Twain

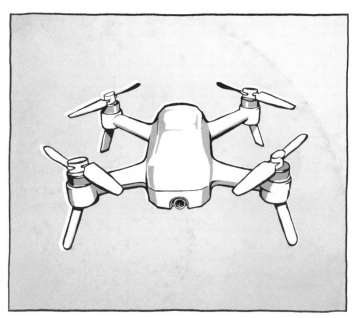
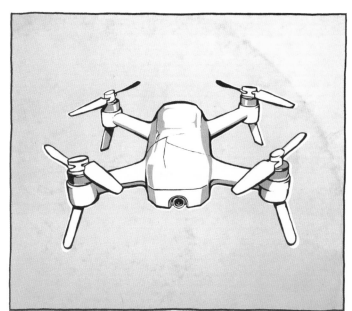
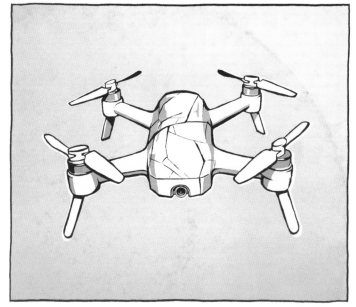

MR.FISH

ONE HUNDRED YEARS OF SOLITUDE

Gabriel García Márquez

ILLUSTRATION BY SIRI DOKKEN

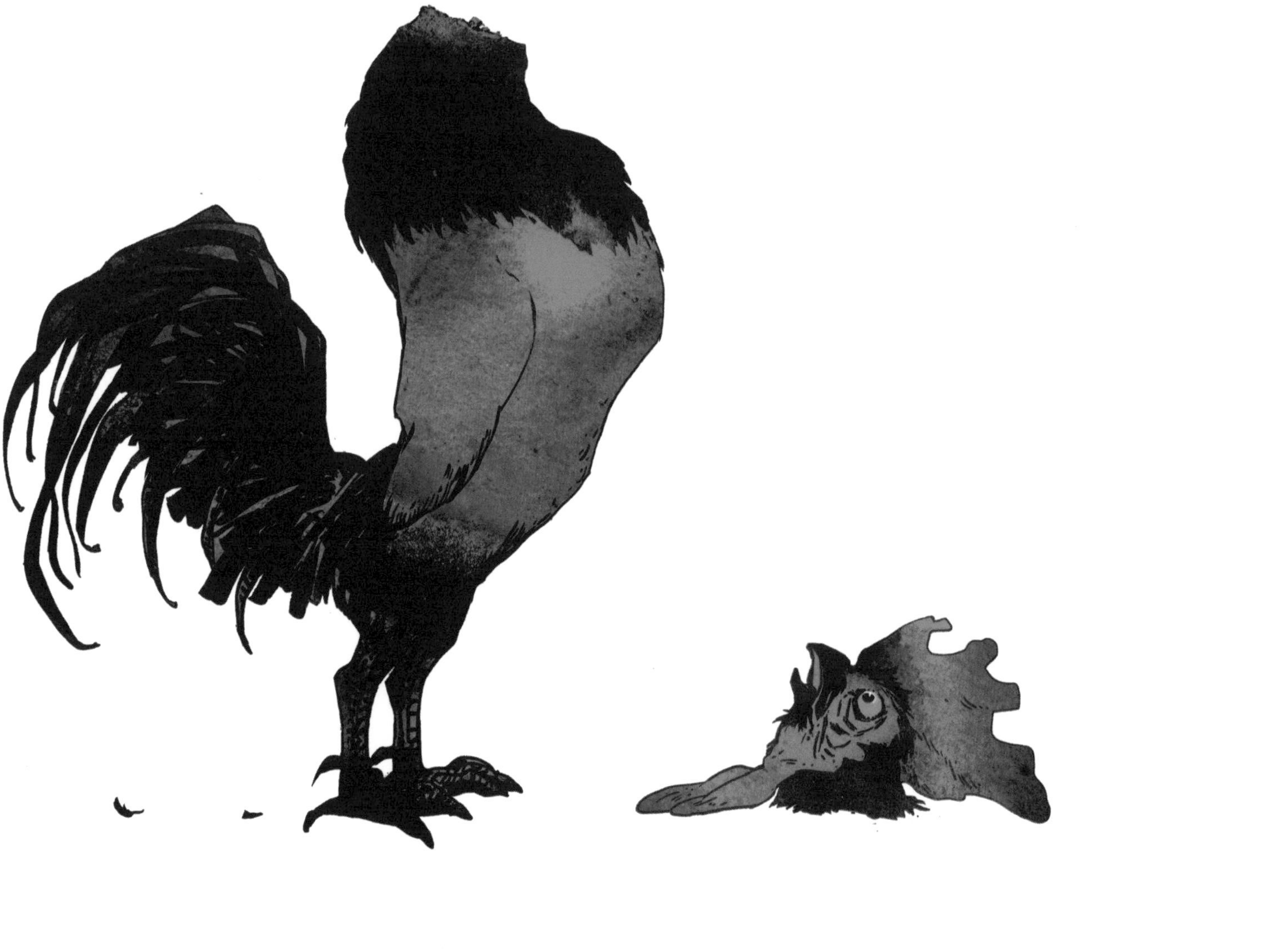

UNDERSTANDING MEDIA
Marshall McLuhan

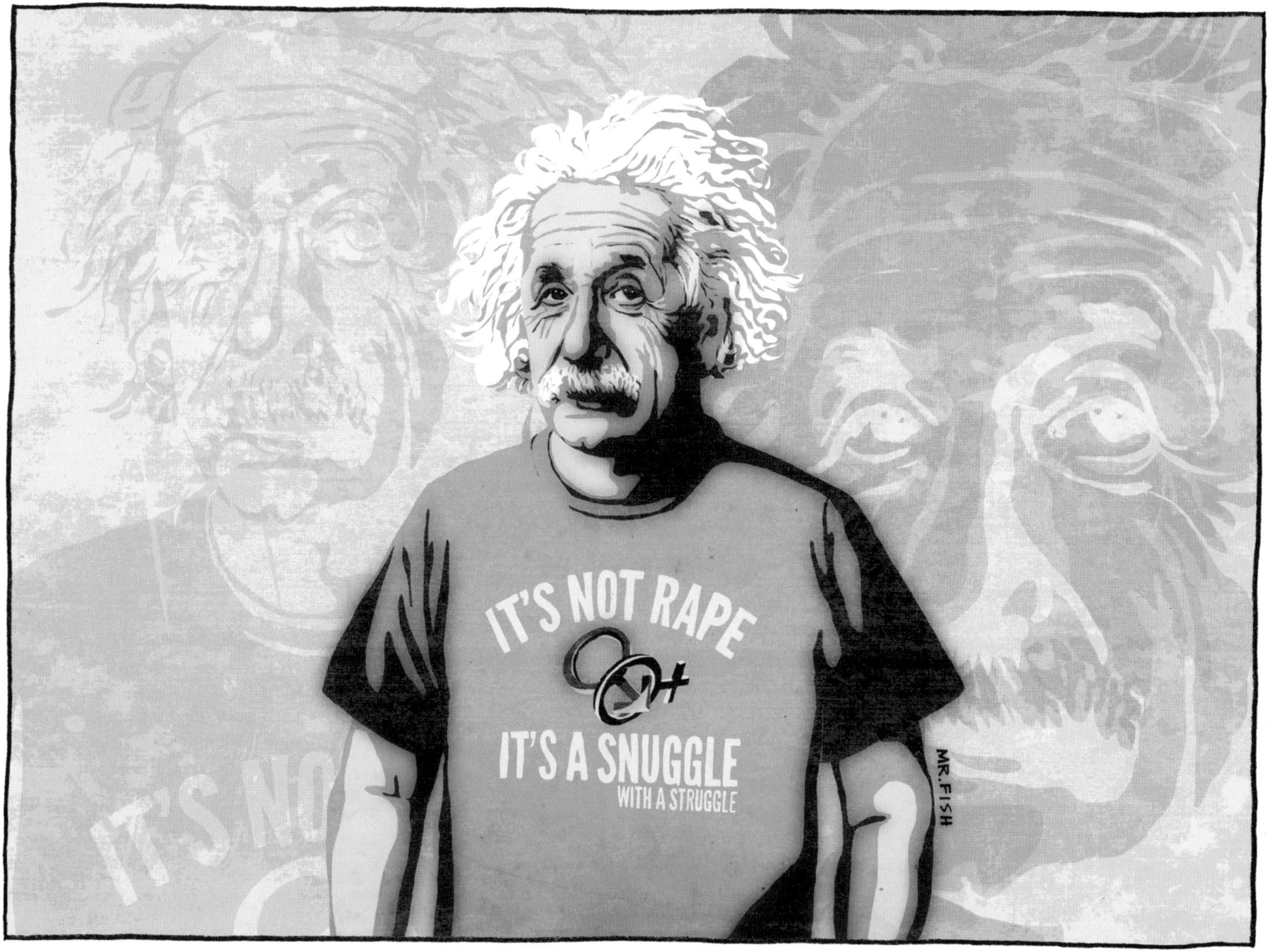
IT'S NOT RAPE
IT'S A SNUGGLE
WITH A STRUGGLE
MR. FISH

HEART OF DARKNESS

Joseph Conrad

ILLUSTRATION BY JOHN G.

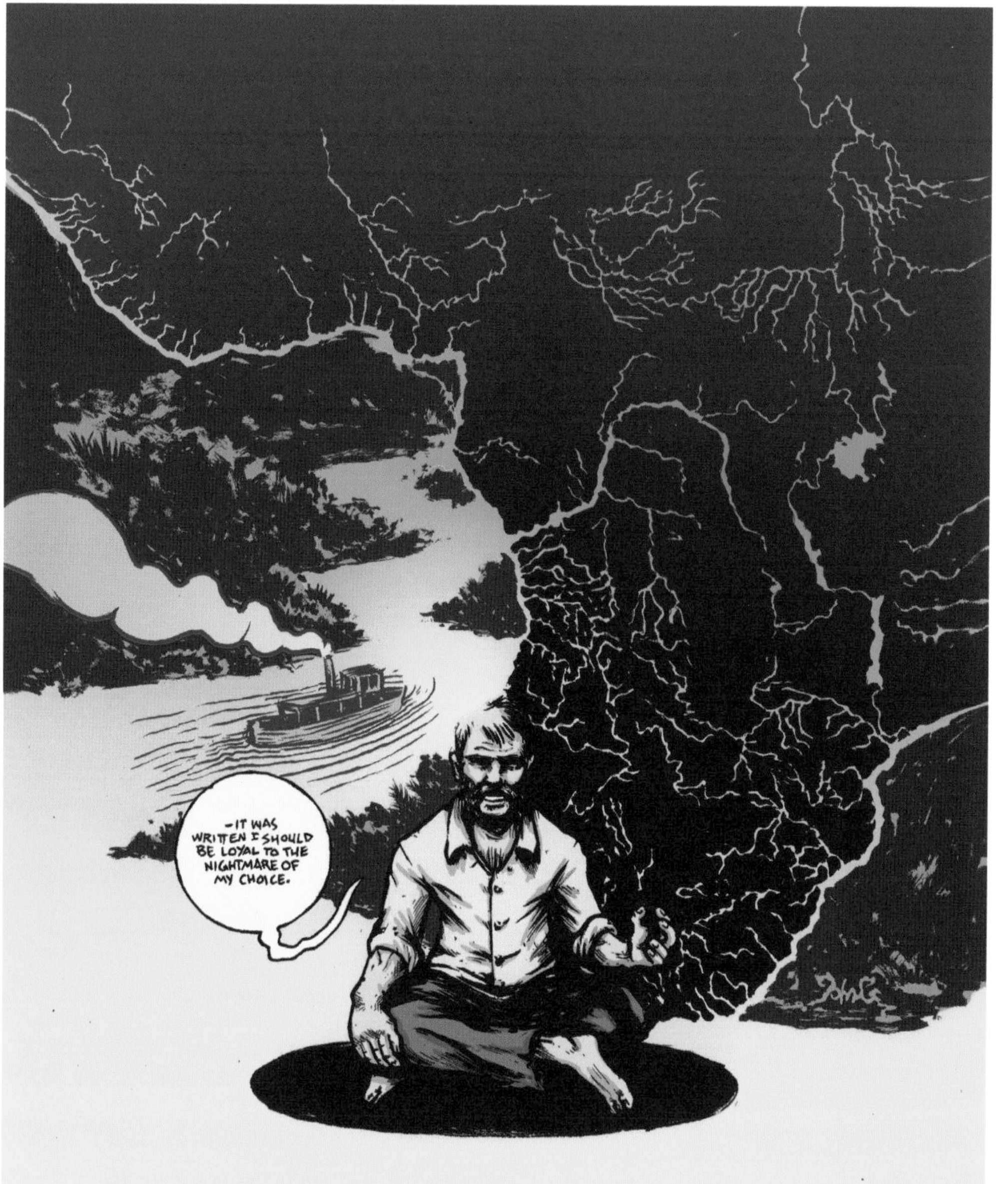
-IT WAS WRITTEN I SHOULD BE LOYAL TO THE NIGHTMARE OF MY CHOICE.

THE WIND-UP BIRD CHRONICLE

Haruki Murakami

ILLUSTRATION BY ANDY SINGER

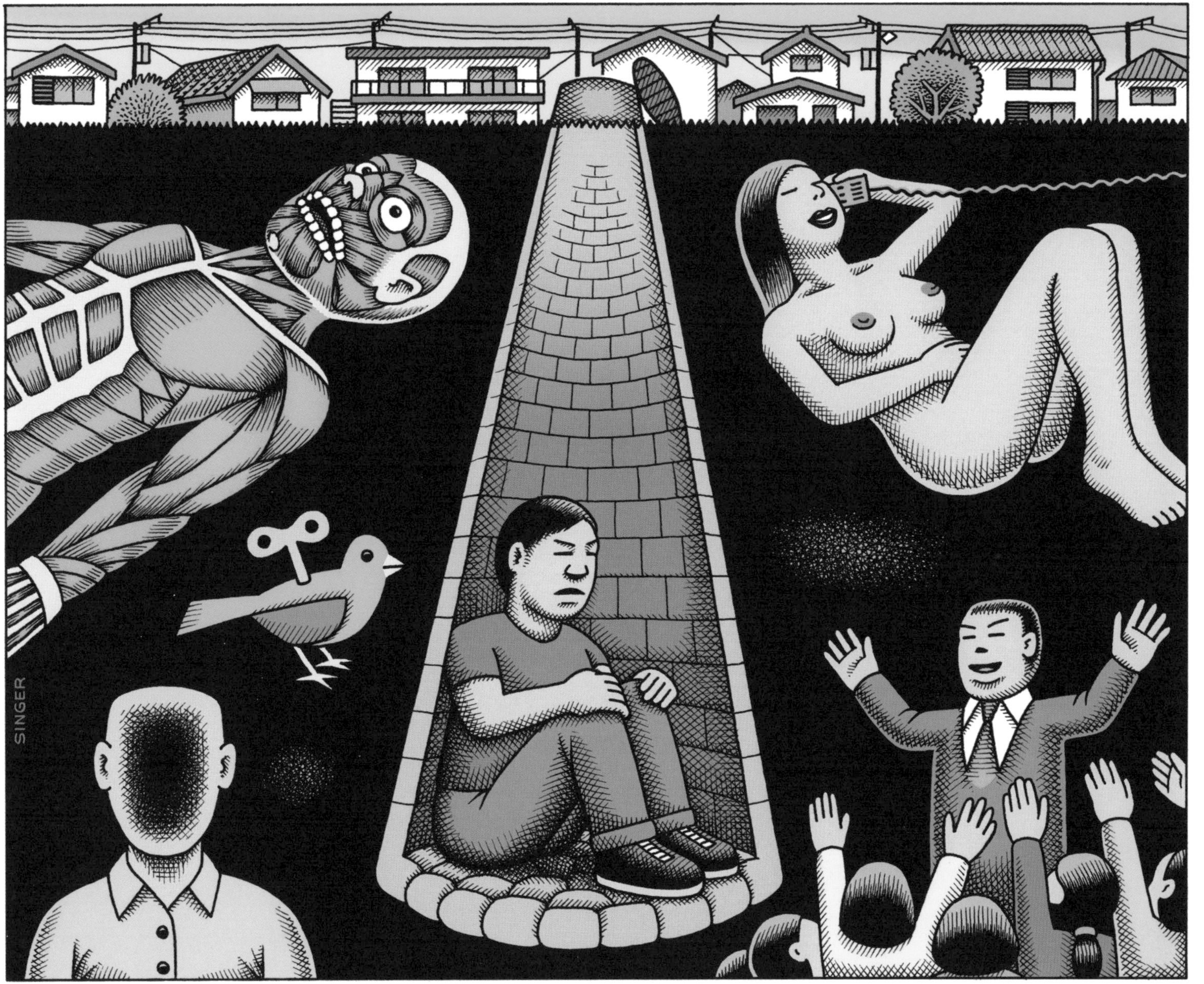
SINGER

ROMEO AND JULIET

William Shakespeare

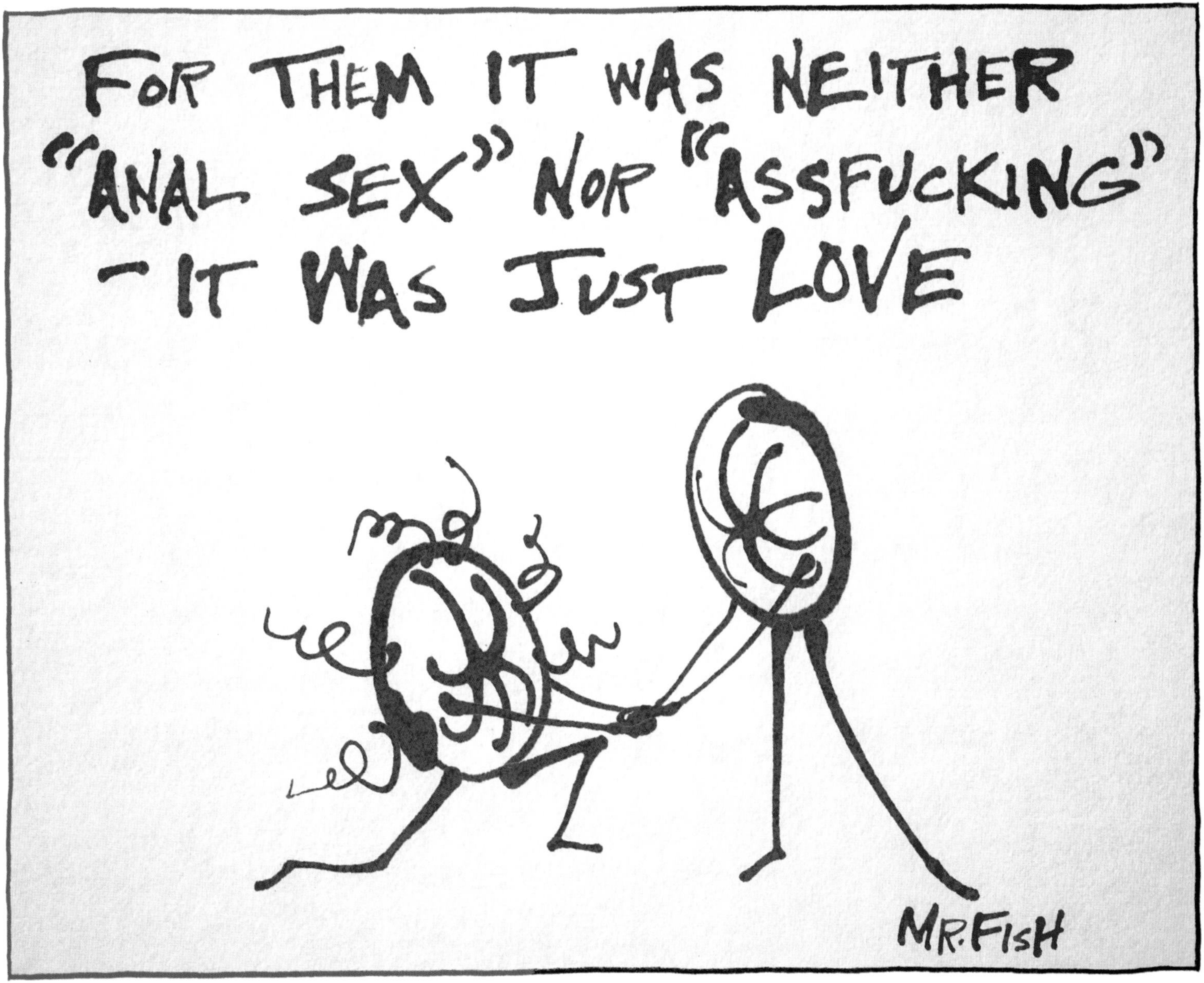
FOR THEM IT WAS NEITHER "ANAL SEX" NOR "ASSFUCKING" – IT WAS JUST LOVE
MR. FISH

DON QUIXOTE

Miguel de Cervantes

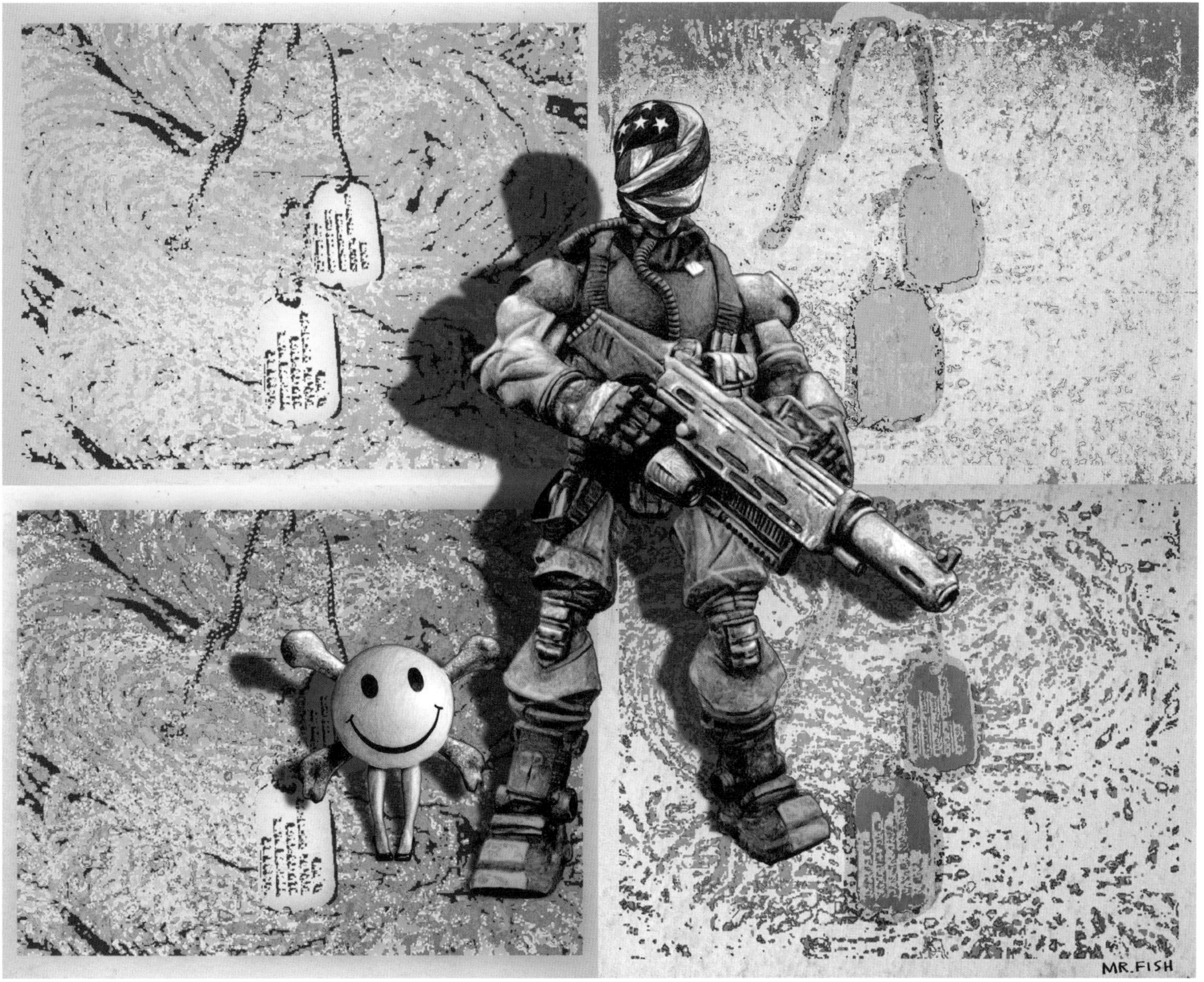
MR. FISH

HARRY POTTER

J. K. Rowling

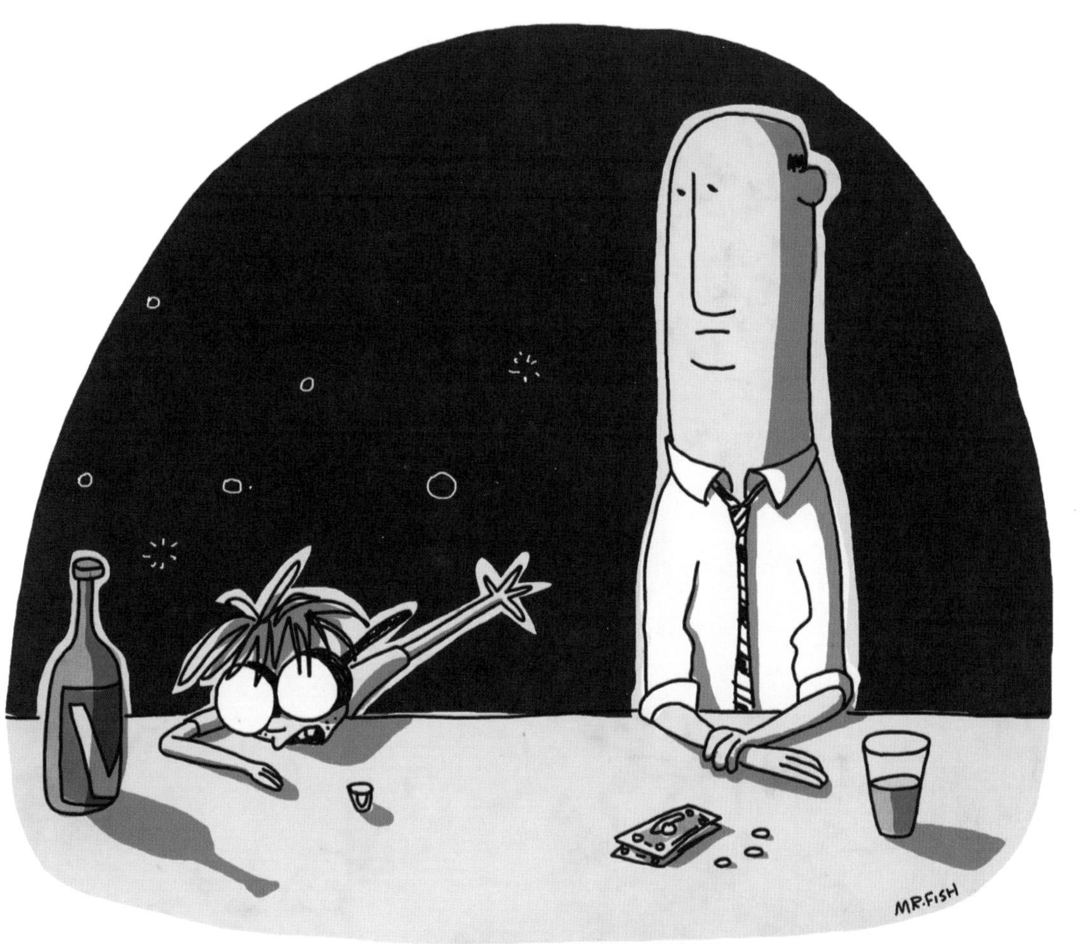
MR.FISH

"This fucking bottle killed my parents and gave me a gnarly-ass scar! Not only that, it turns perfectly reasonable people into complete assholes! I hate it! I really fucking hate it—but it's got its hooks in me deep! And you know what? I have to tell you, I feel like a complete shithead because it's taken me my whole life to realize that, yeah, sure, I'm fucking amazing on the shit, but I'm not that bottle—I'm ME! You get what I'm saying, mister? I'm Harry—just plain fucking scar-face Harry."

ANNA KARENINA
Leo Tolstoy

ILLUSTRATION BY TARA SEIBEL

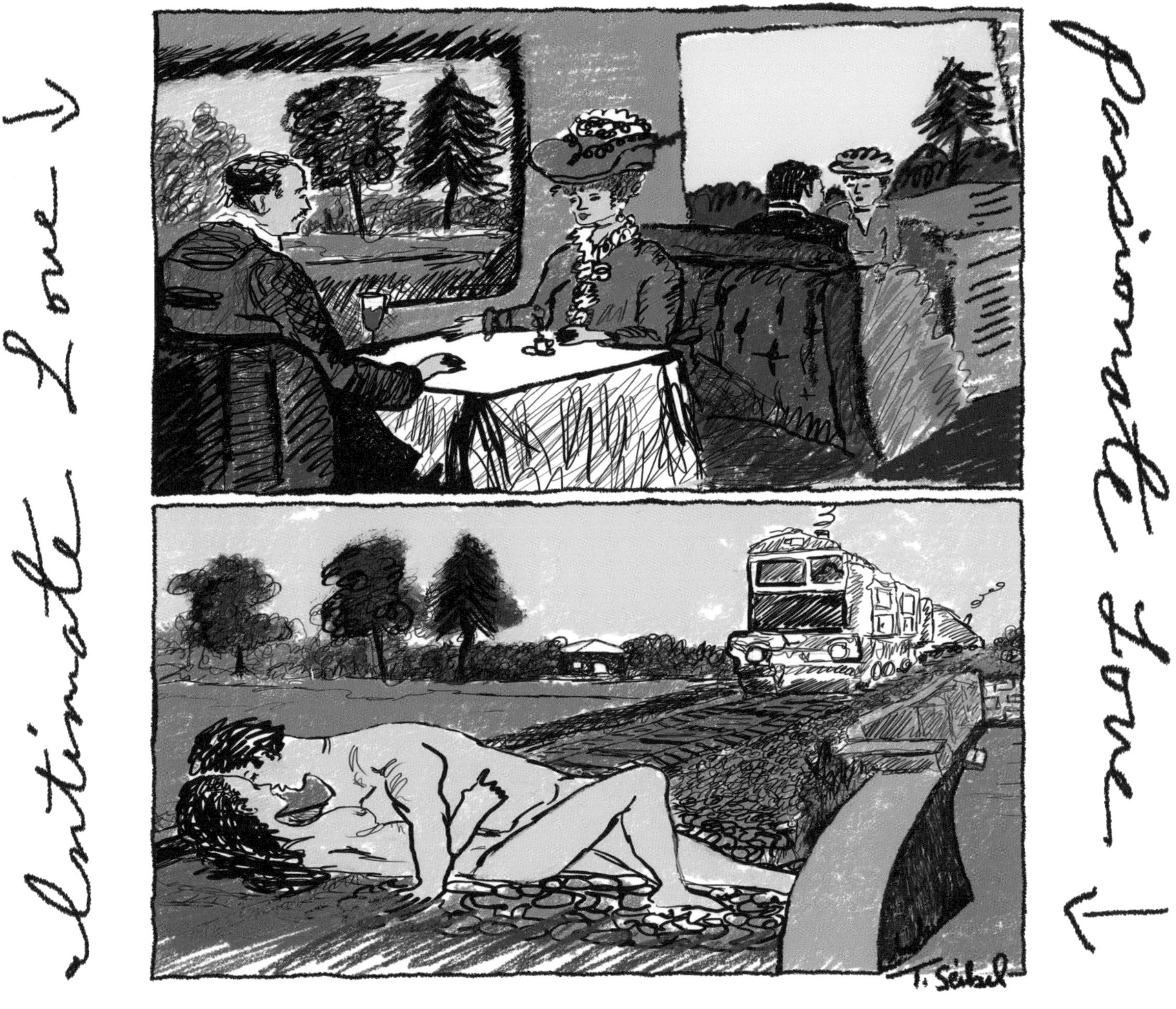
Intimate Love
Passionate Love
T. Seibel

INVISIBLE MAN

Ralph Ellison

ILLUSTRATION BY GARY DUMM

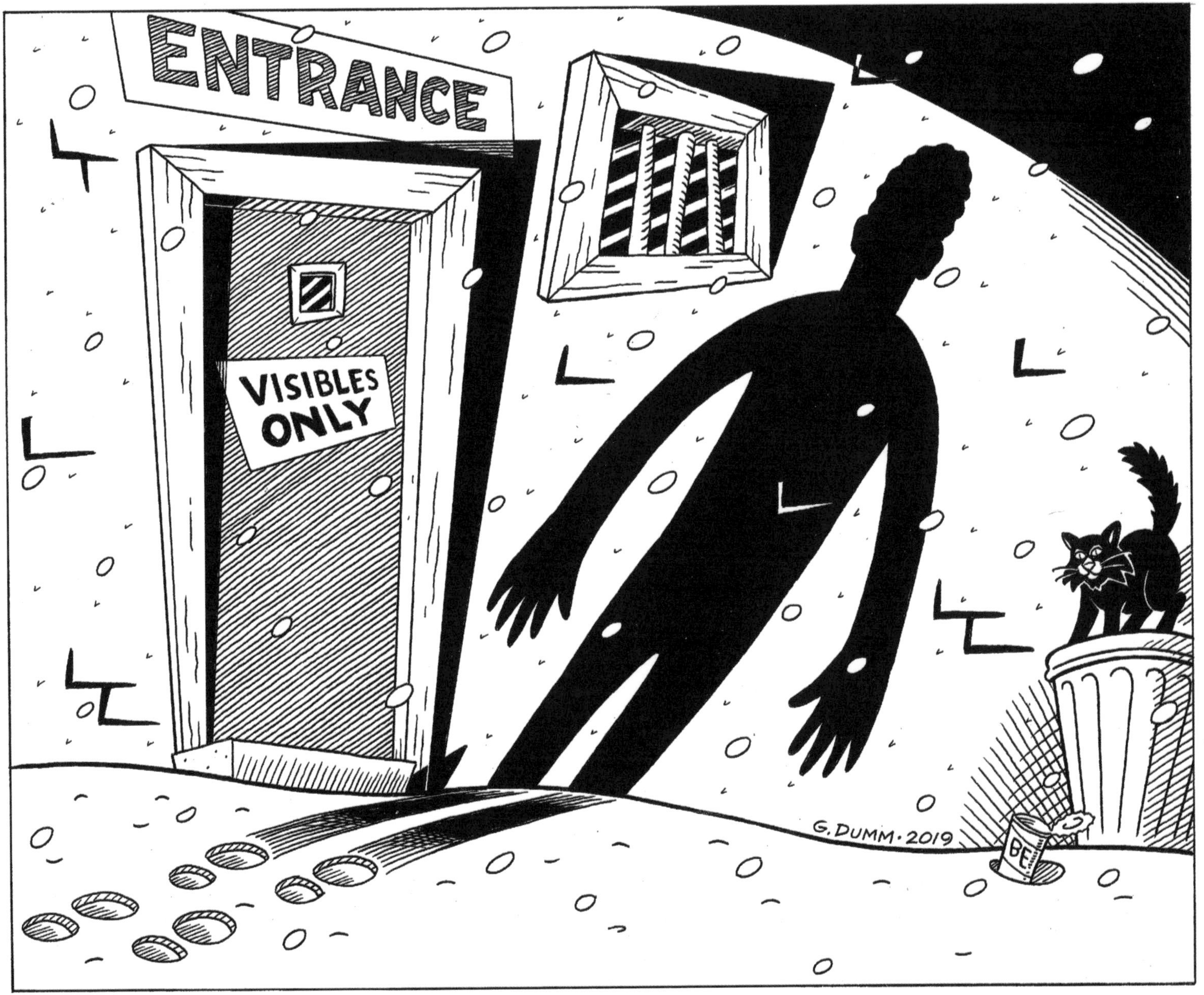
ENTRANCE
VISIBLES ONLY
G. DUMM · 2019

A PEOPLE'S HISTORY OF THE UNITED STATES
Howard Zinn

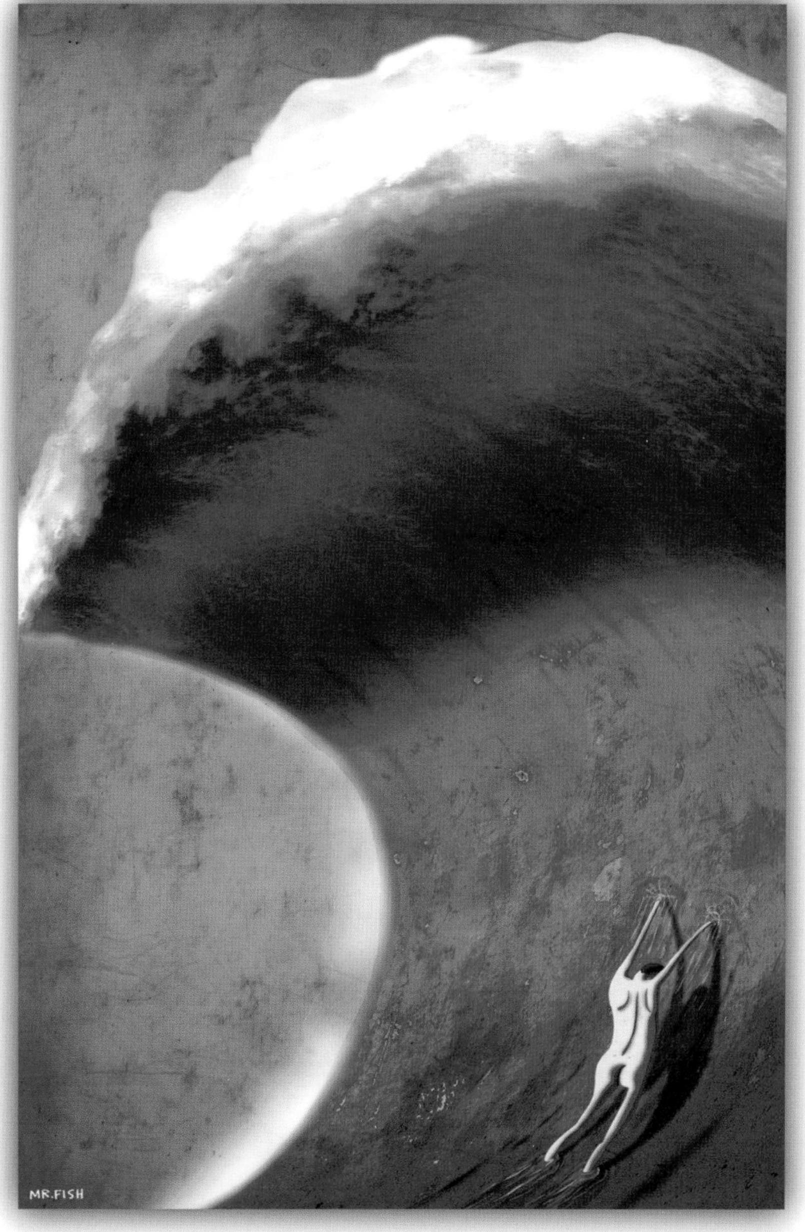
MR.FISH

THE STRANGER
Albert Camus

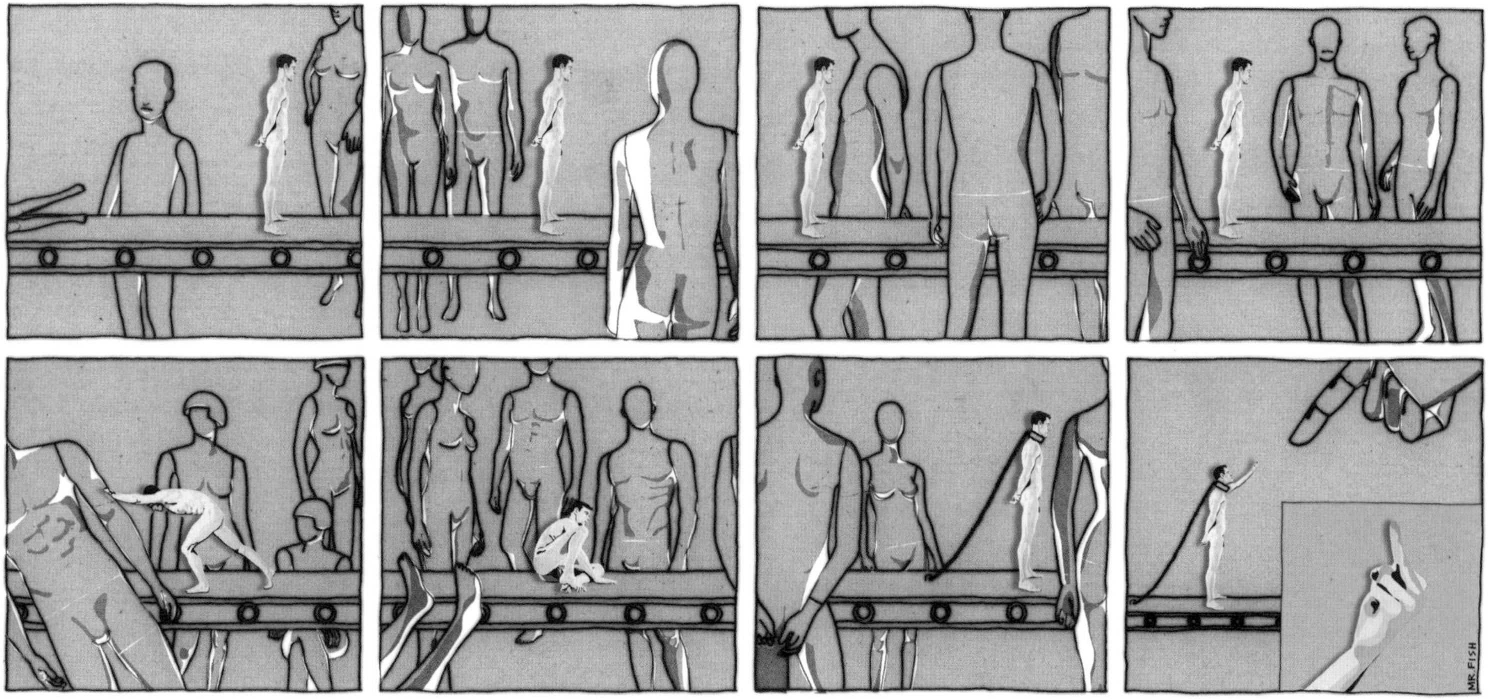
MR.FISH

A BOY'S OWN STORY

Edmund White

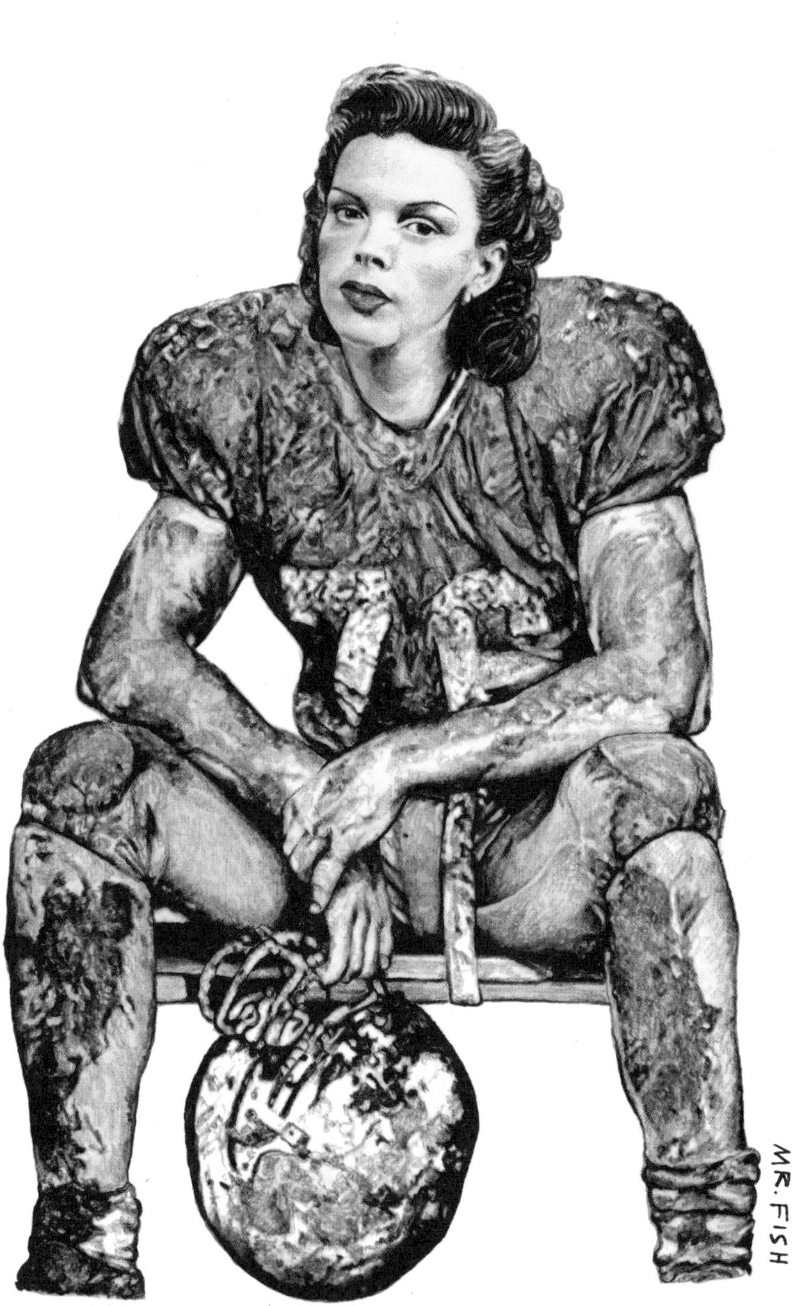
MR. FISH

A CONFEDERACY OF DUNCES
John Kennedy Toole

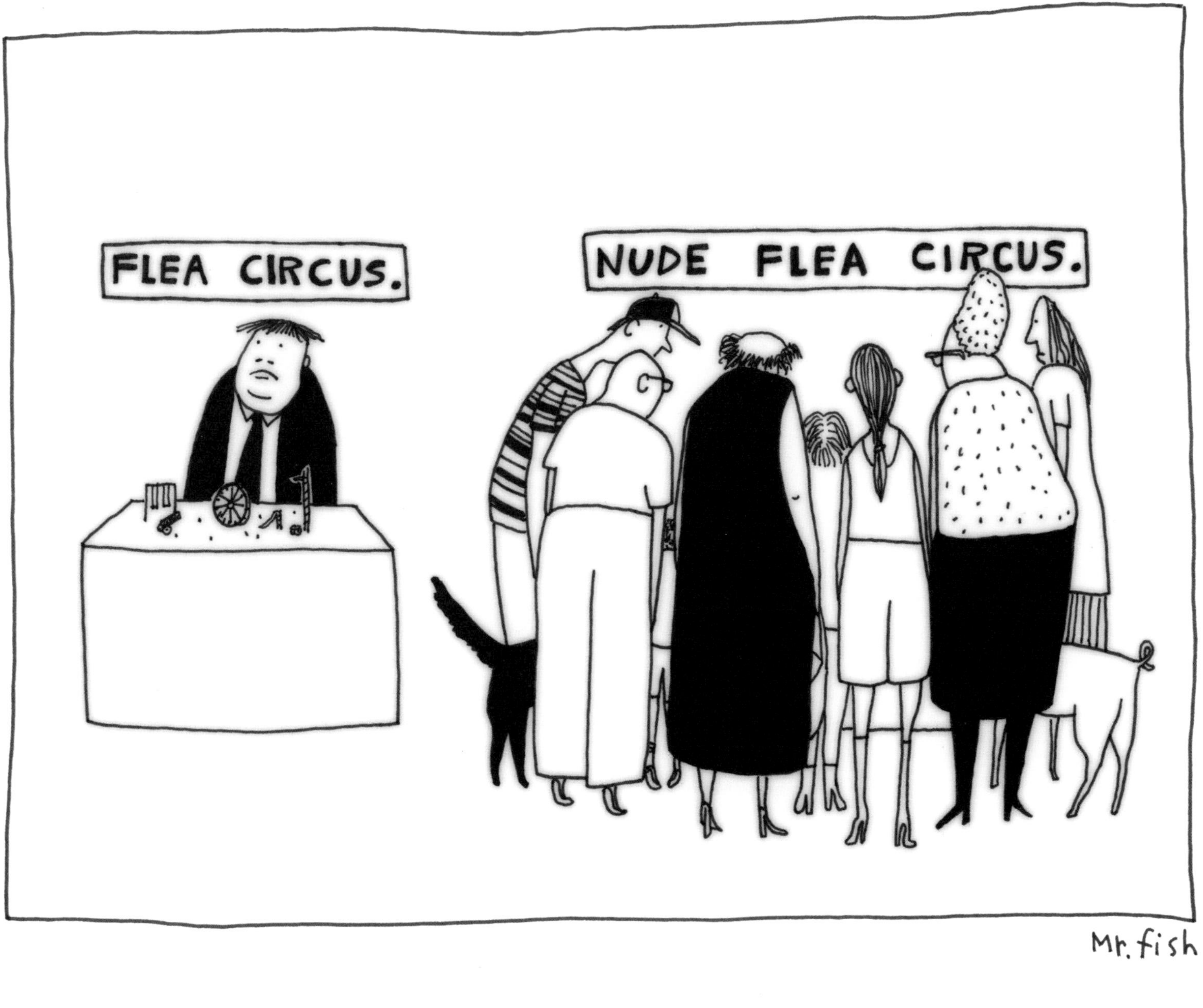
FLEA CIRCUS.
NUDE FLEA CIRCUS.
Mr. fish

ANIMAL FARM

George Orwell

ILLUSTRATION BY CLARE KOLAT

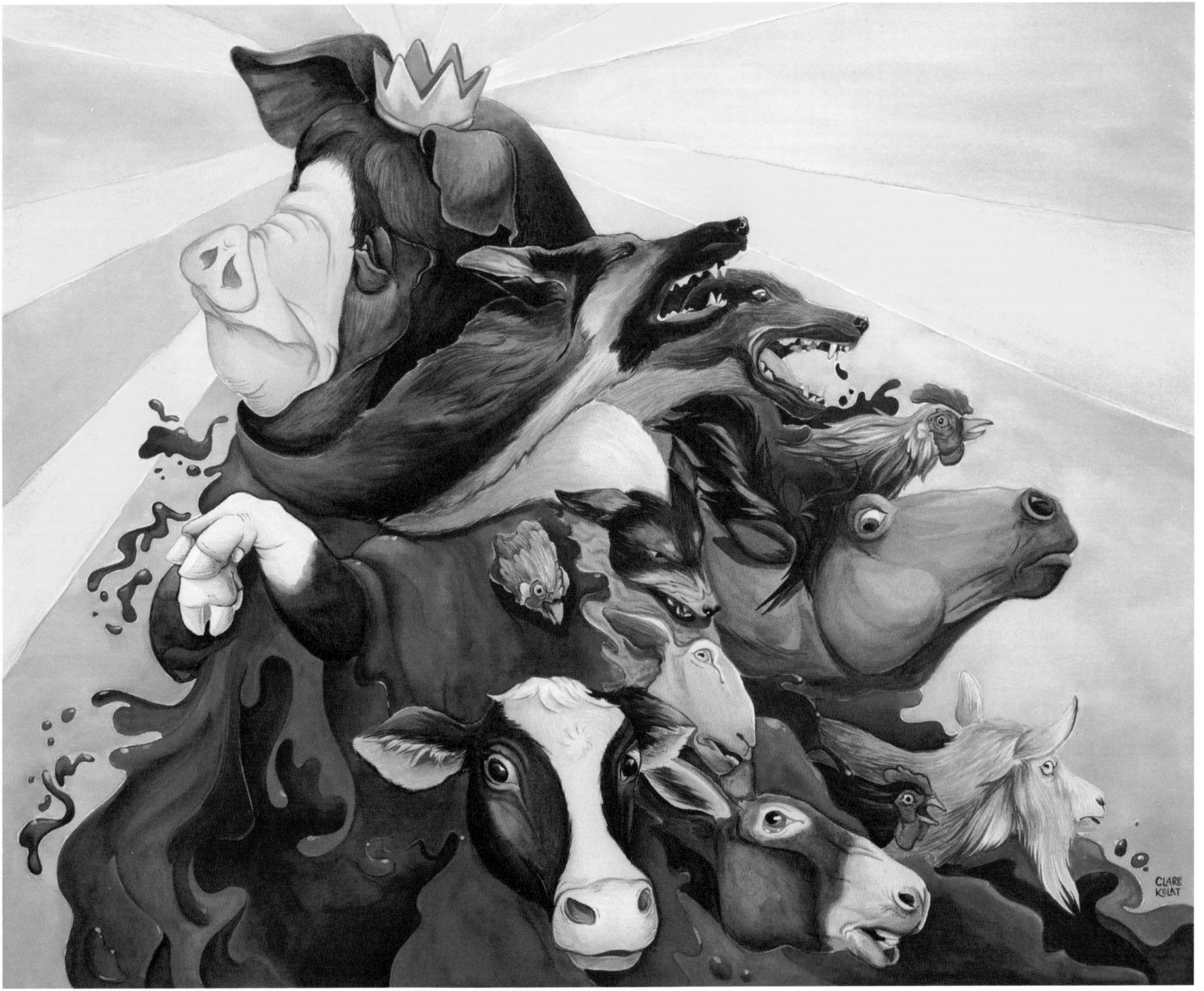
CLARE
KOLAT

PARADISE LOST

John Milton

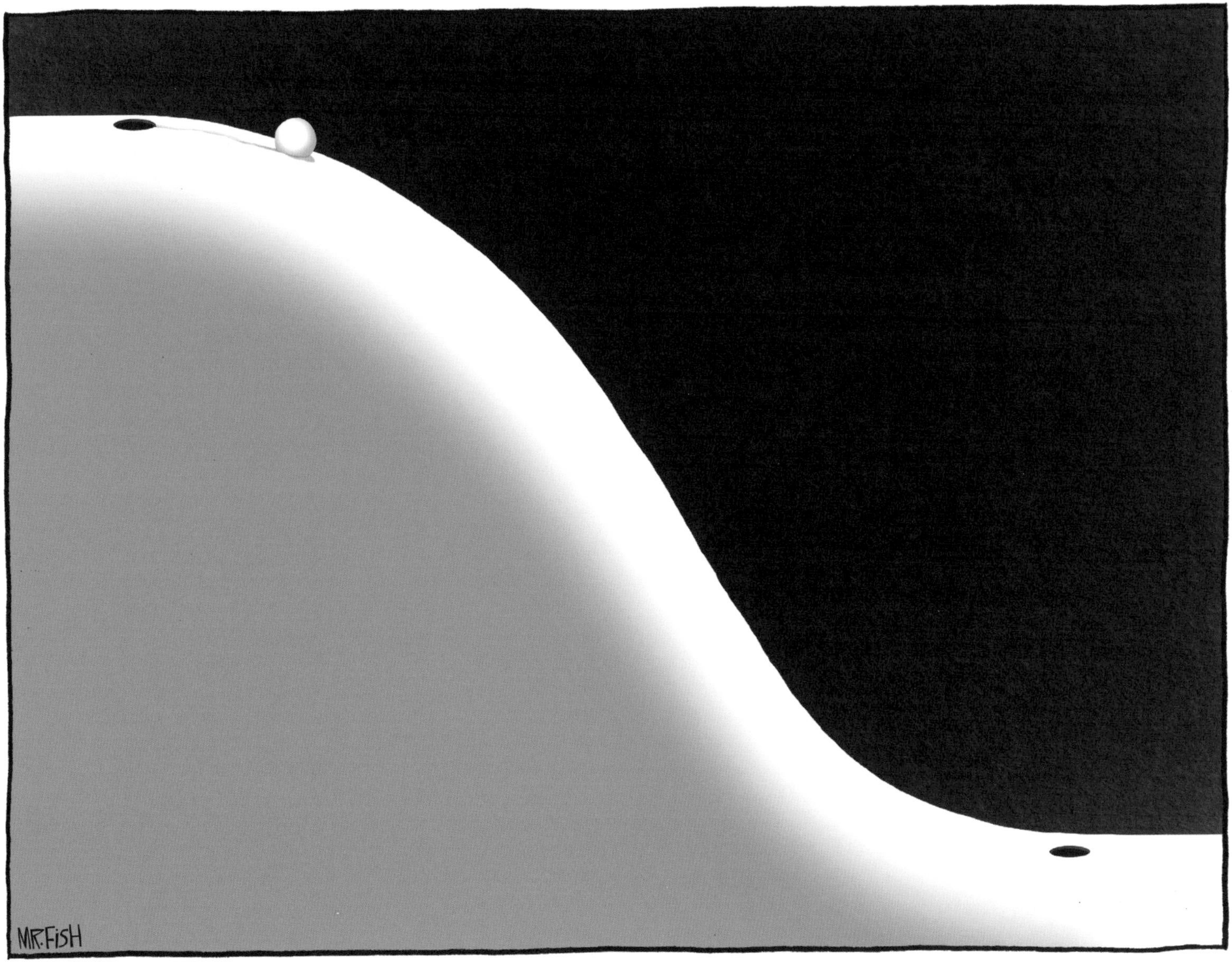
MR. FISH

HOWL

Allen Ginsberg

TREVOR RECEIVING HIS GRANT APPLICATION FROM THE NEA.

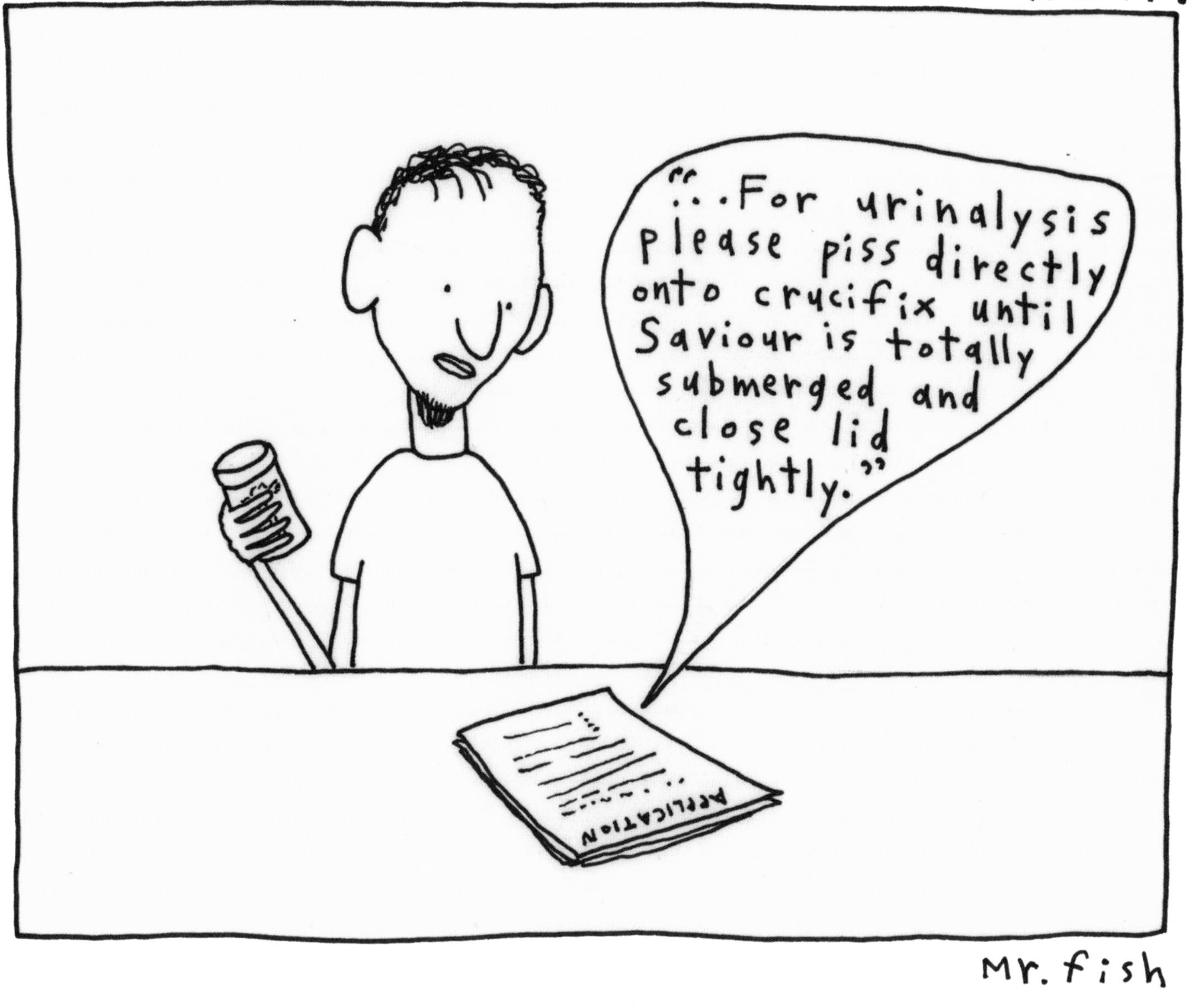
"...For urinalysis please piss directly onto crucifix until Saviour is totally submerged and close lid tightly."
APPLICATION
mr. fish

METAMORPHOSES (PYGMALION)
Ovid

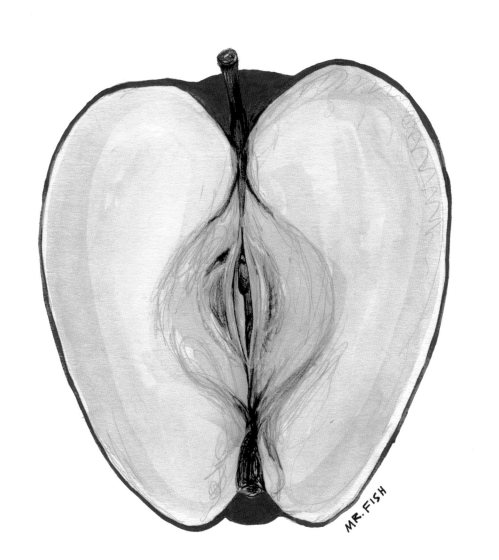

MR. FISH

THE MAN WHO DIED

D. H. Lawrence

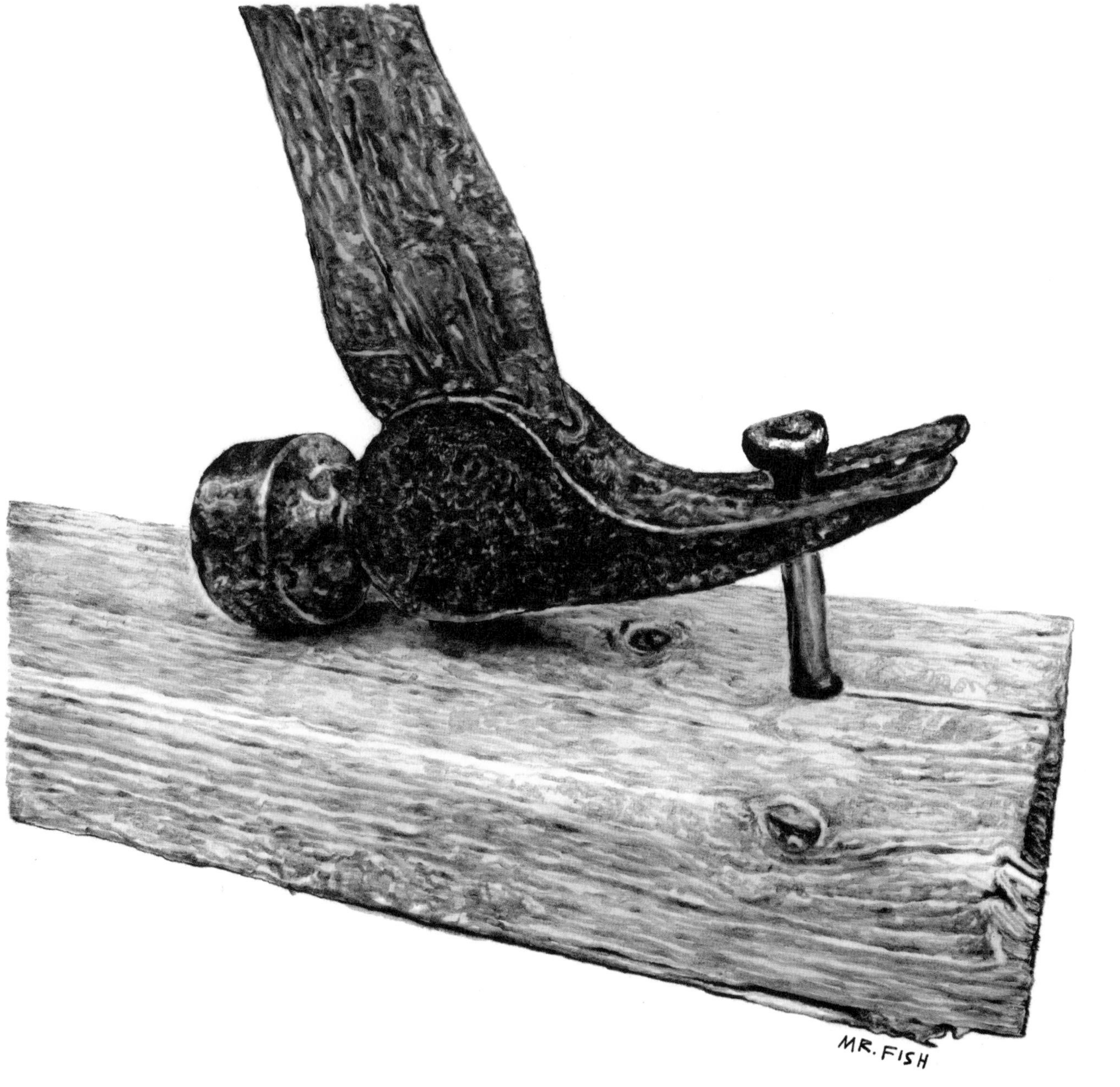
MR. FISH

TALES OF ORDINARY MADNESS

Charles Bukowski

ILLUSTRATION BY NATE ULSH

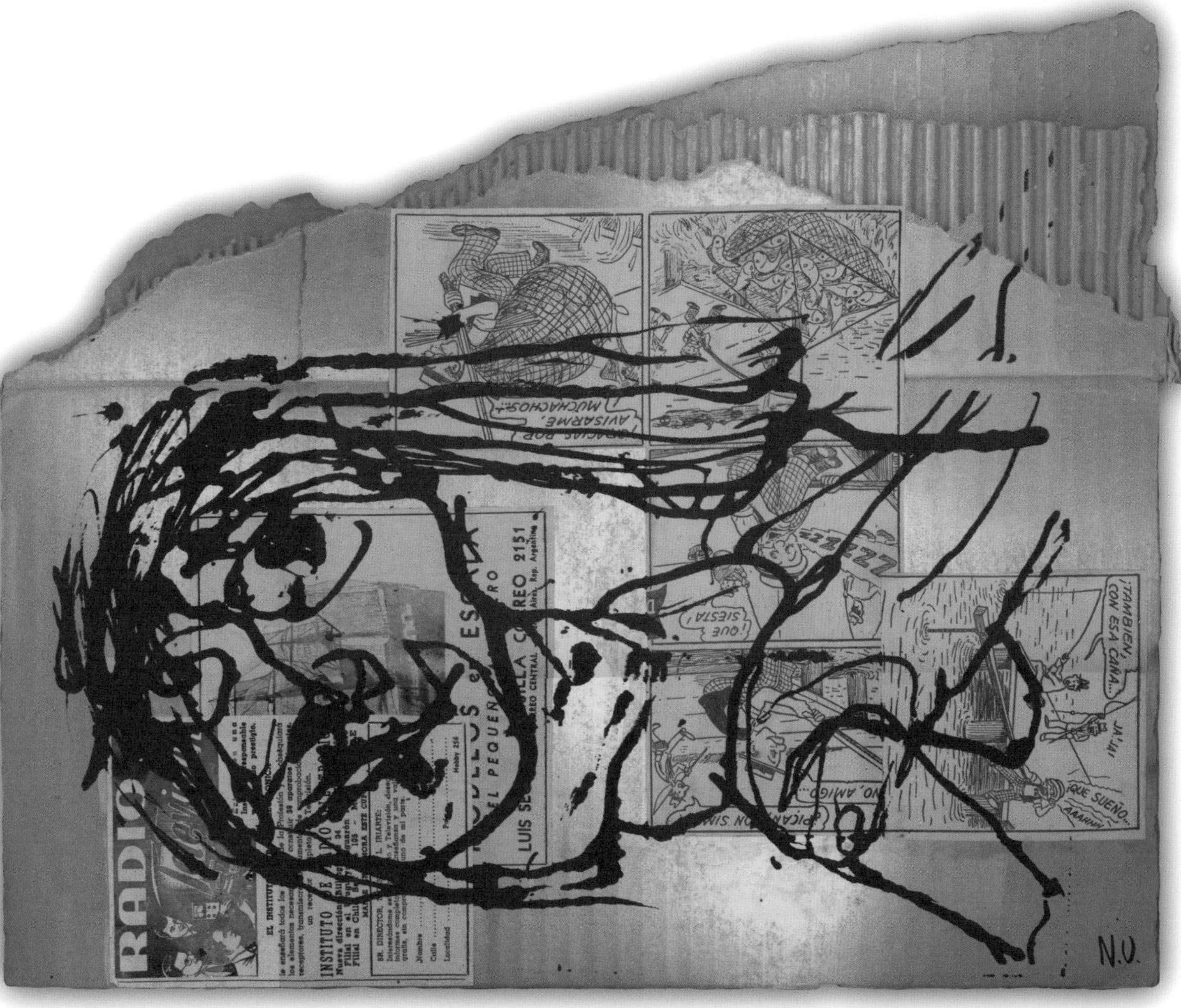

¡TAMBIEN, CON ESA CAÑA...
JA, JA!
¡QUE SUEÑO...
AAAHHH
NO, AMIGO...
¡QUE SIESTA!
AVISARME, MUCHACHOS!
CASILLA CORREO 2151
RADIO
INSTITUTO
N.U.

OEDIPUS REX

Sophocles

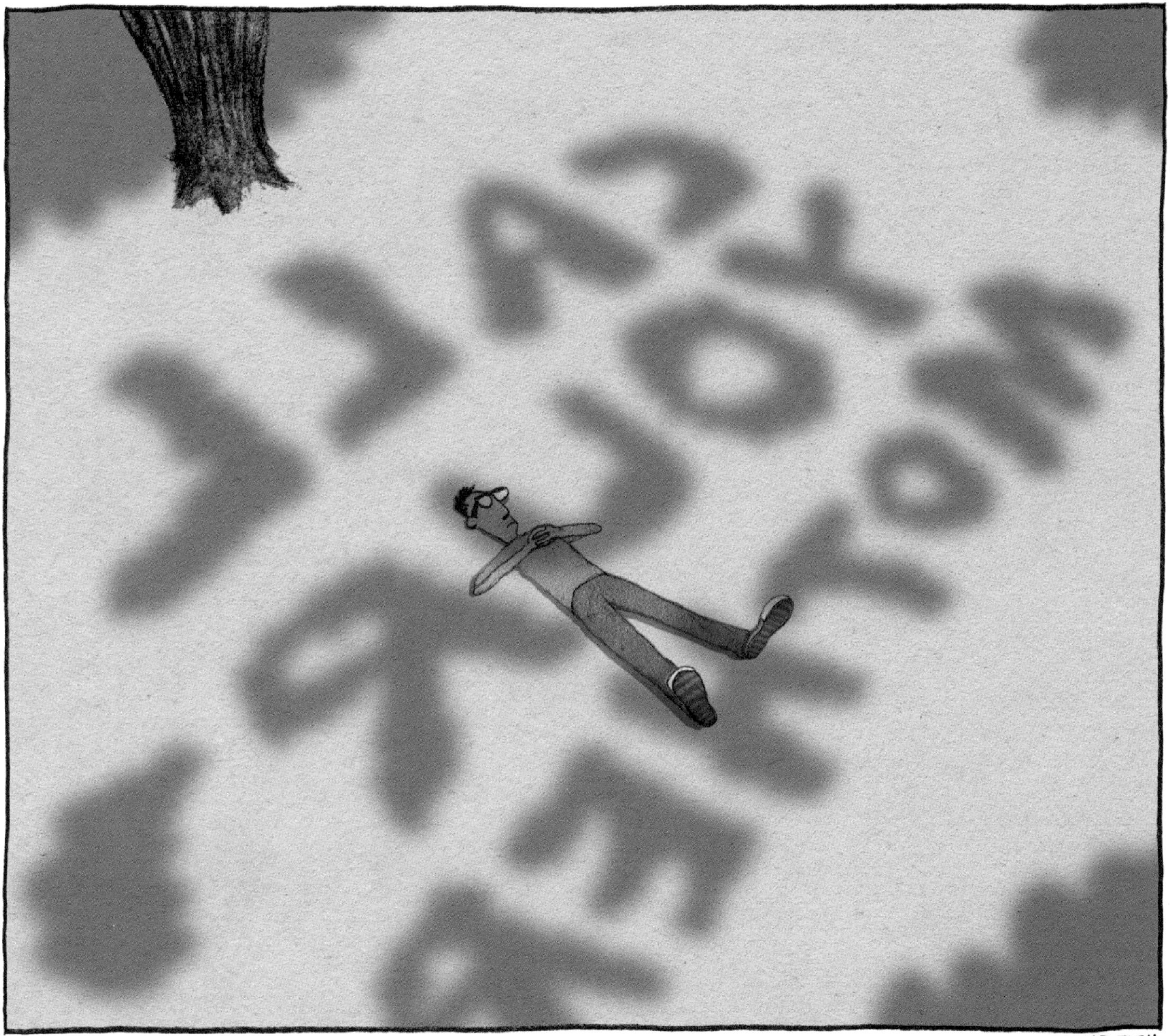

MR.FISH

FAHRENHEIT 451

Ray Bradbury

ILLUSTRATION BY BENJAMIN SLYNGSTAD

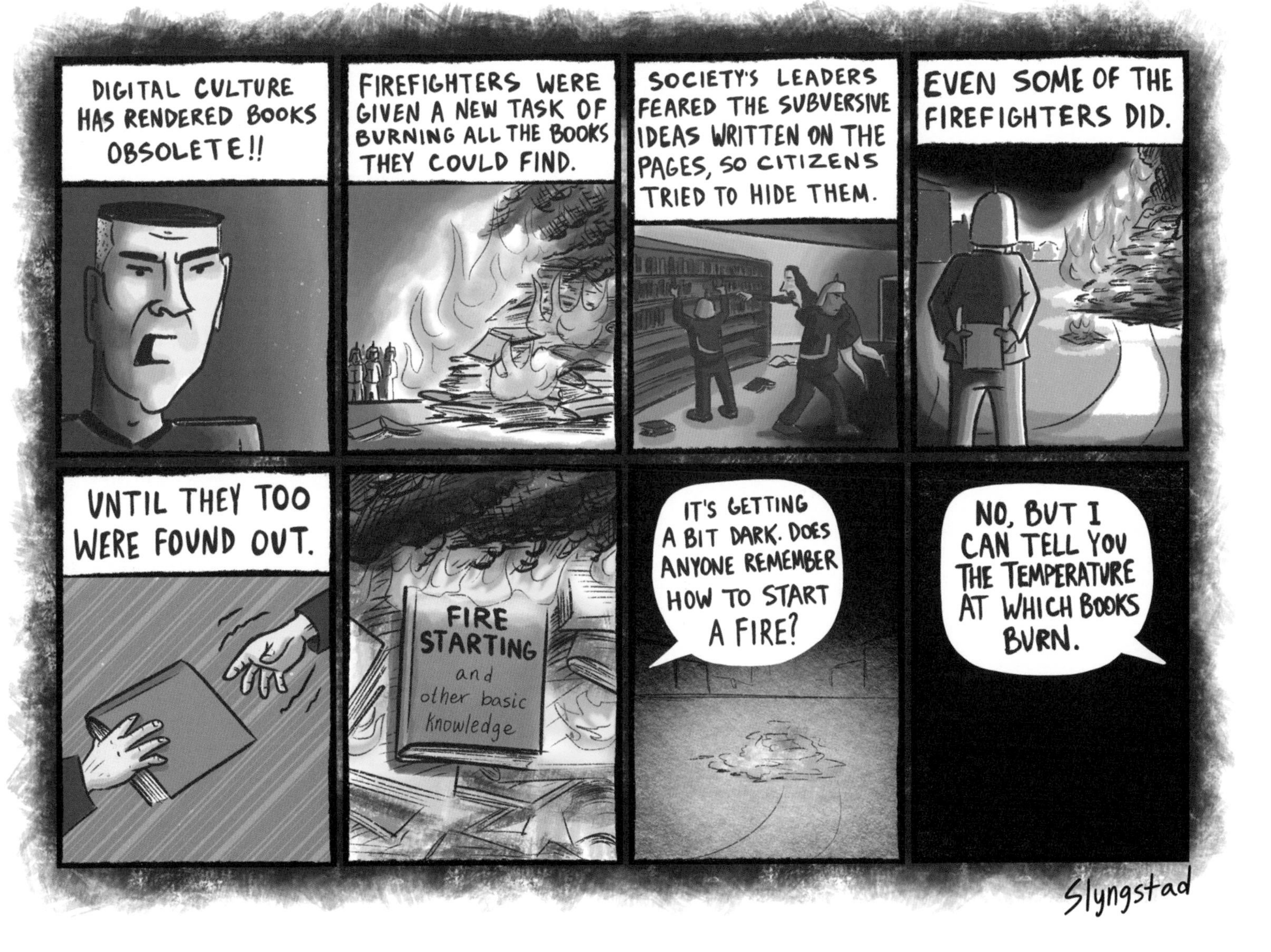
DIGITAL CULTURE HAS RENDERED BOOKS OBSOLETE!!
FIREFIGHTERS WERE GIVEN A NEW TASK OF BURNING ALL THE BOOKS THEY COULD FIND.
SOCIETY'S LEADERS FEARED THE SUBVERSIVE IDEAS WRITTEN ON THE PAGES, SO CITIZENS TRIED TO HIDE THEM.
EVEN SOME OF THE FIREFIGHTERS DID.
UNTIL THEY TOO WERE FOUND OUT.
FIRE STARTING and other basic knowledge
IT'S GETTING A BIT DARK. DOES ANYONE REMEMBER HOW TO START A FIRE?
NO, BUT I CAN TELL YOU THE TEMPERATURE AT WHICH BOOKS BURN.
Slyngstad

CATCH-22

Joseph Heller

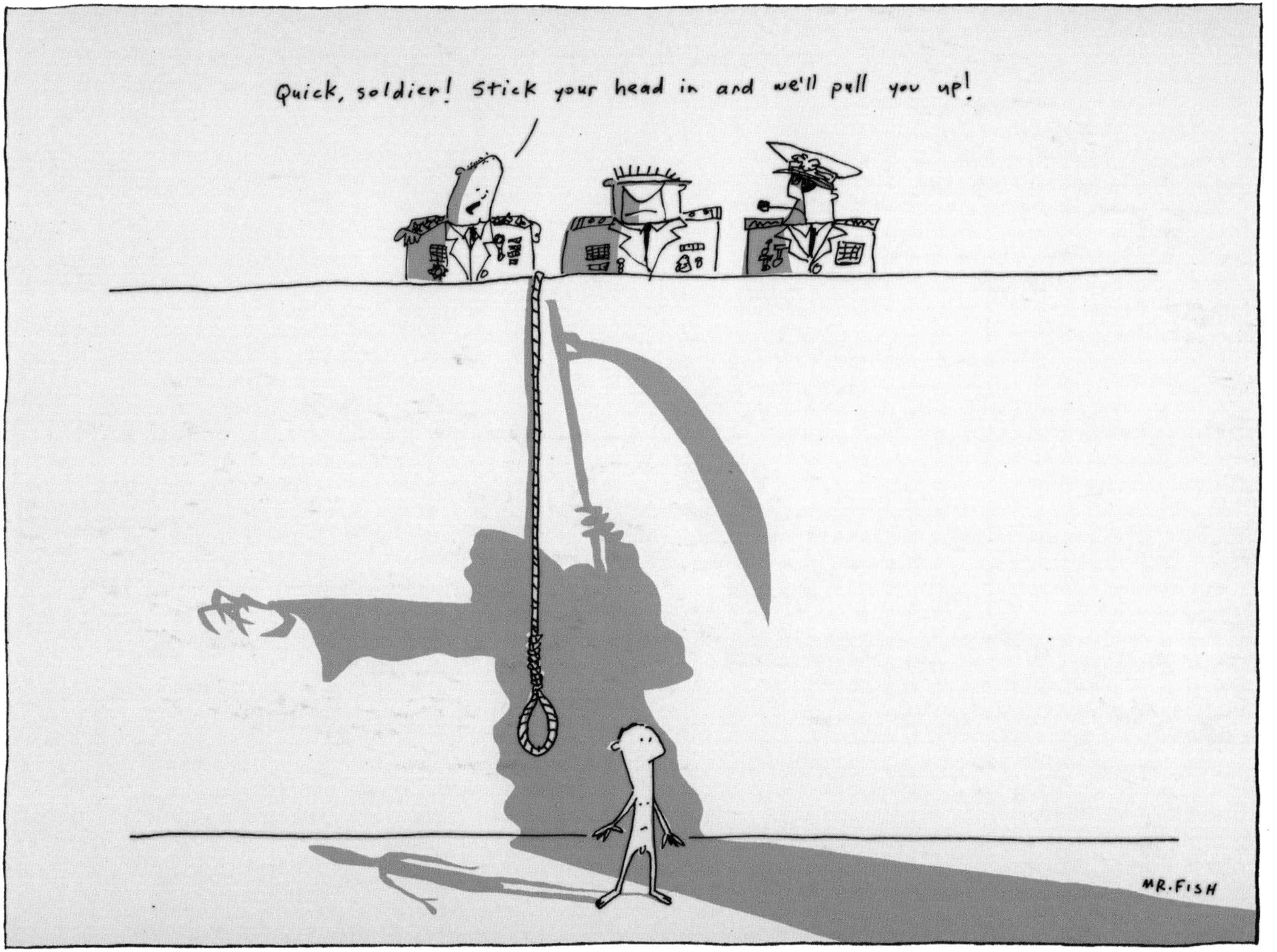
Quick, soldier! Stick your head in and we'll pull you up!
MR. FISH

CIVILIZATION AND ITS DISCONTENTS
Sigmund Freud

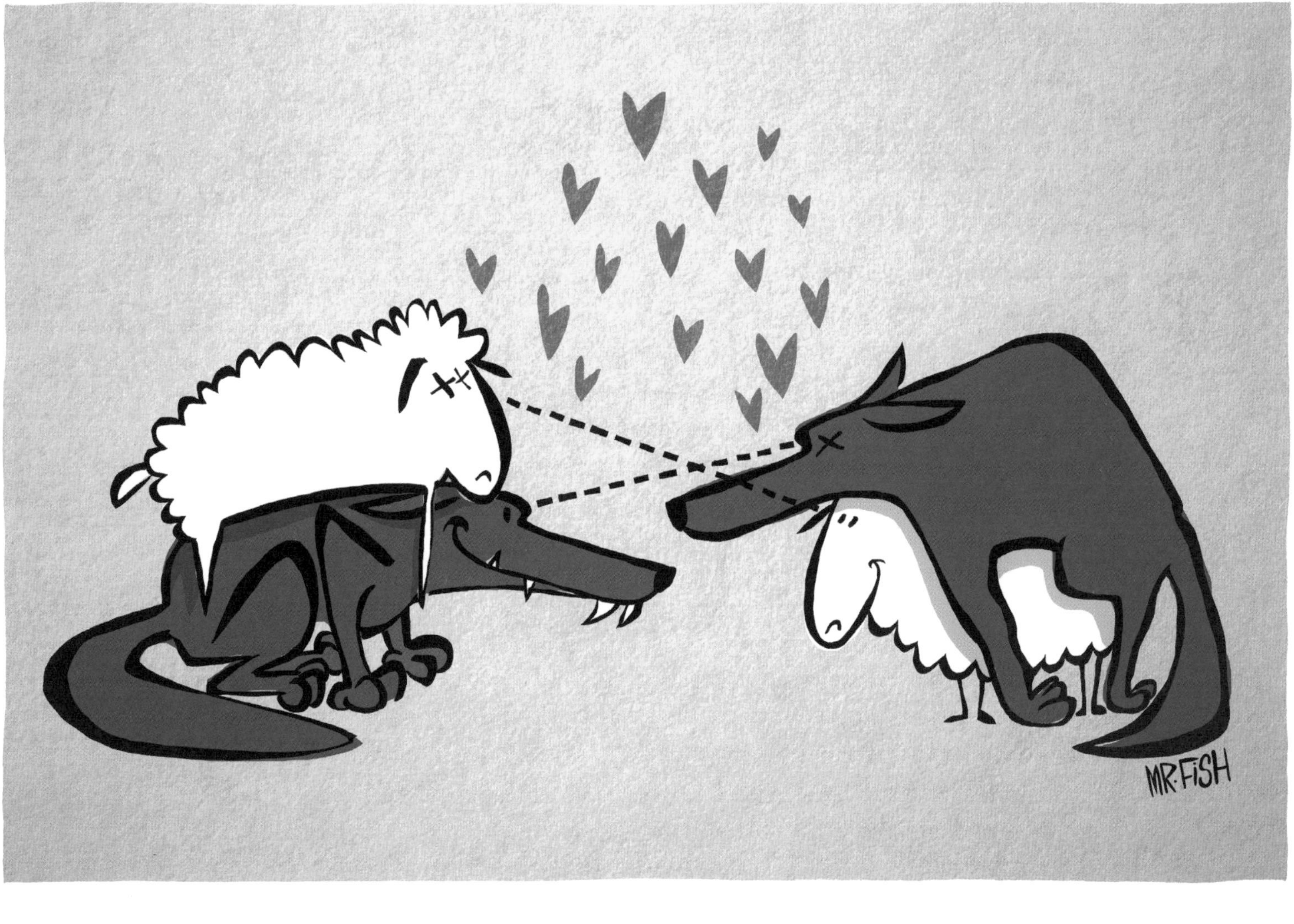
MR. FISH

1984

George Orwell

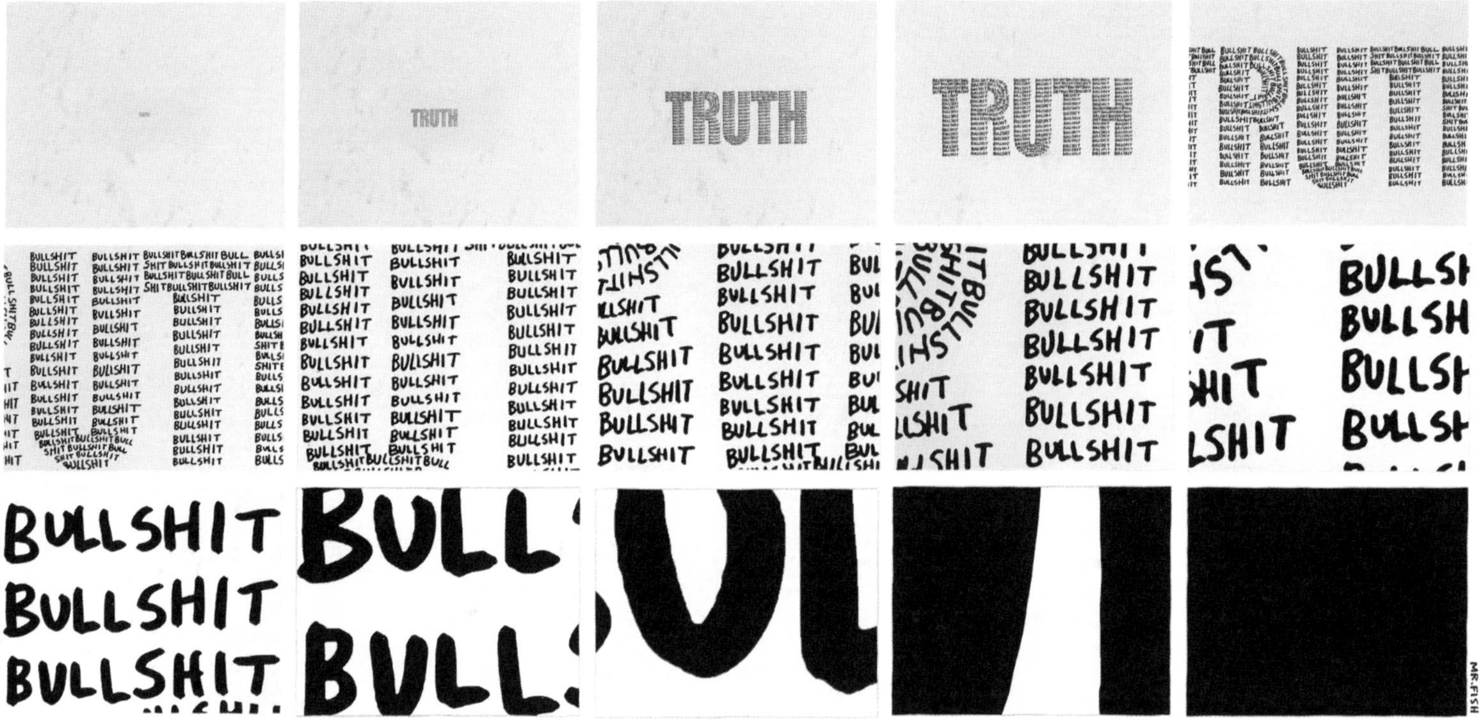
TRUTH
BULLSHIT
MR.FISH

INFINITE JEST

David Foster Wallace

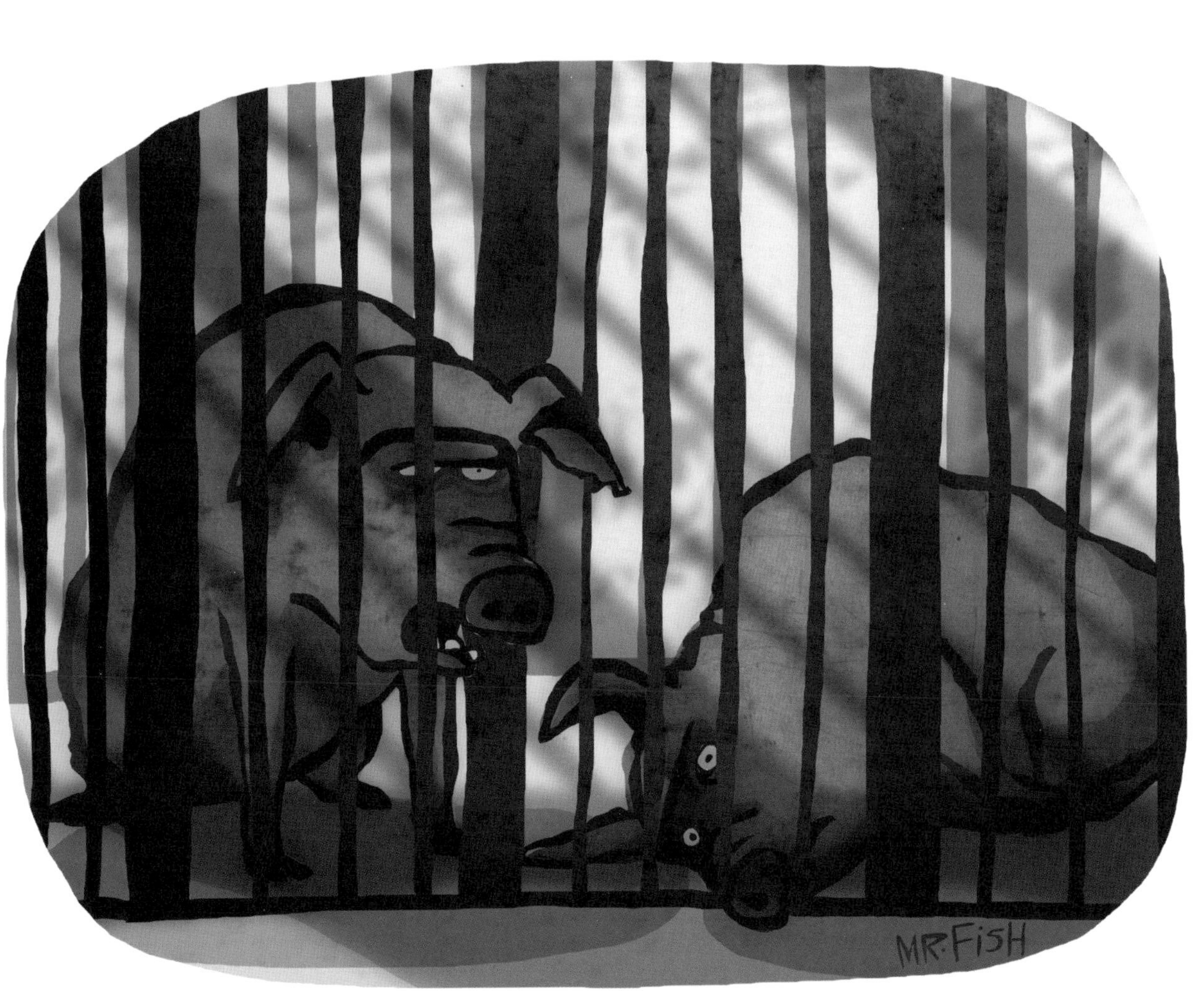
MR.FISH

"Those hippie idiots think they're being so fucking moral for only eating free-range pigs when the truth of the matter is WE'RE the ones who should be put out of our misery. What's so moral about killing an animal that has an actual name, a toy box, that showers regularly and gets to run around outside and chase butterflies and drink in the sunshine? That's a life worth living, assholes! Killing us would be proof that you give a goddamn shit about mercy!"

THE OLD MAN AND THE SEA

Ernest Hemingway

ILLUSTRATION BY RON HILL

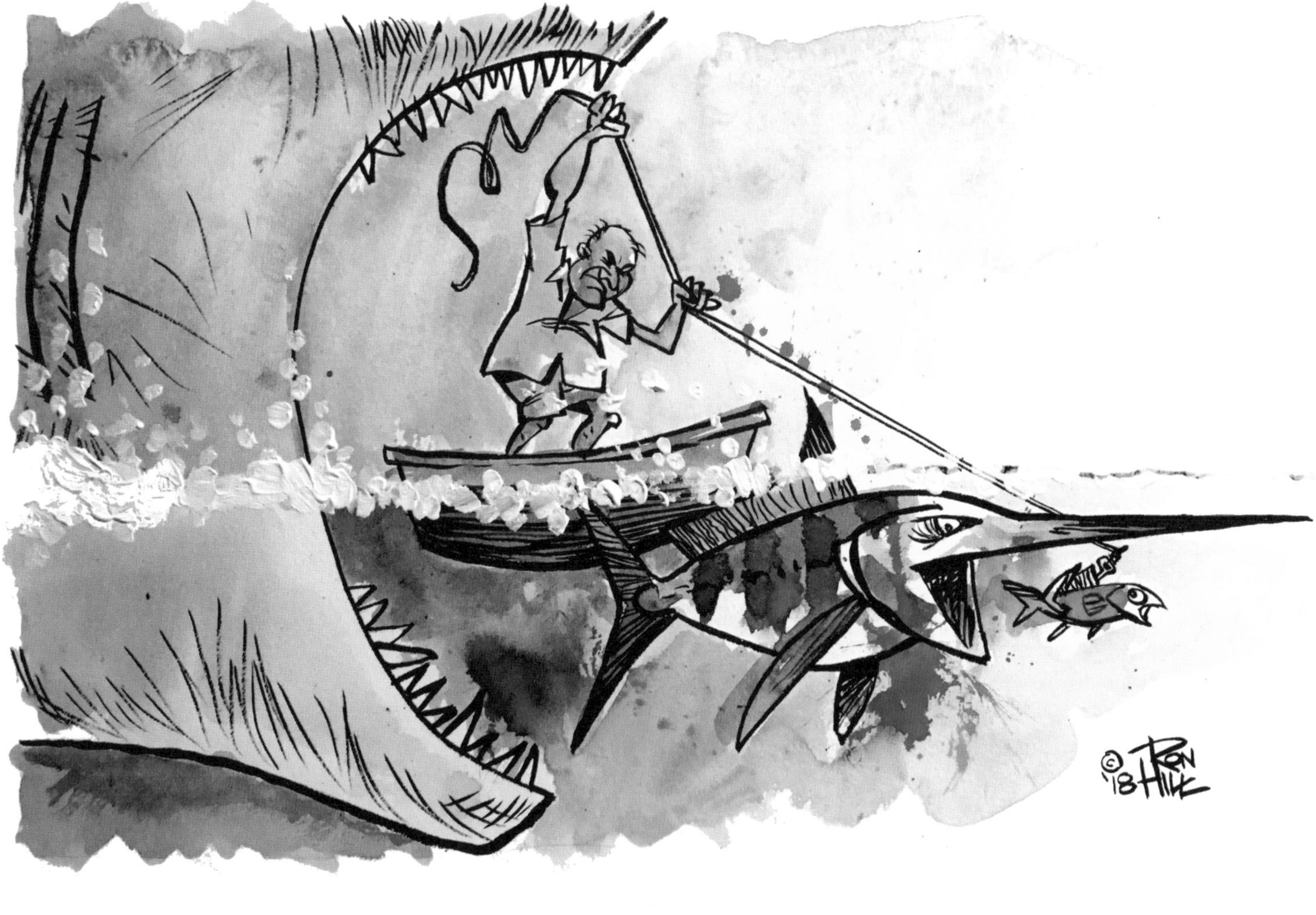
© '18 RON HILL

THE ARMIES OF THE NIGHT
Norman Mailer

THE WISHBONE OF A DOVE

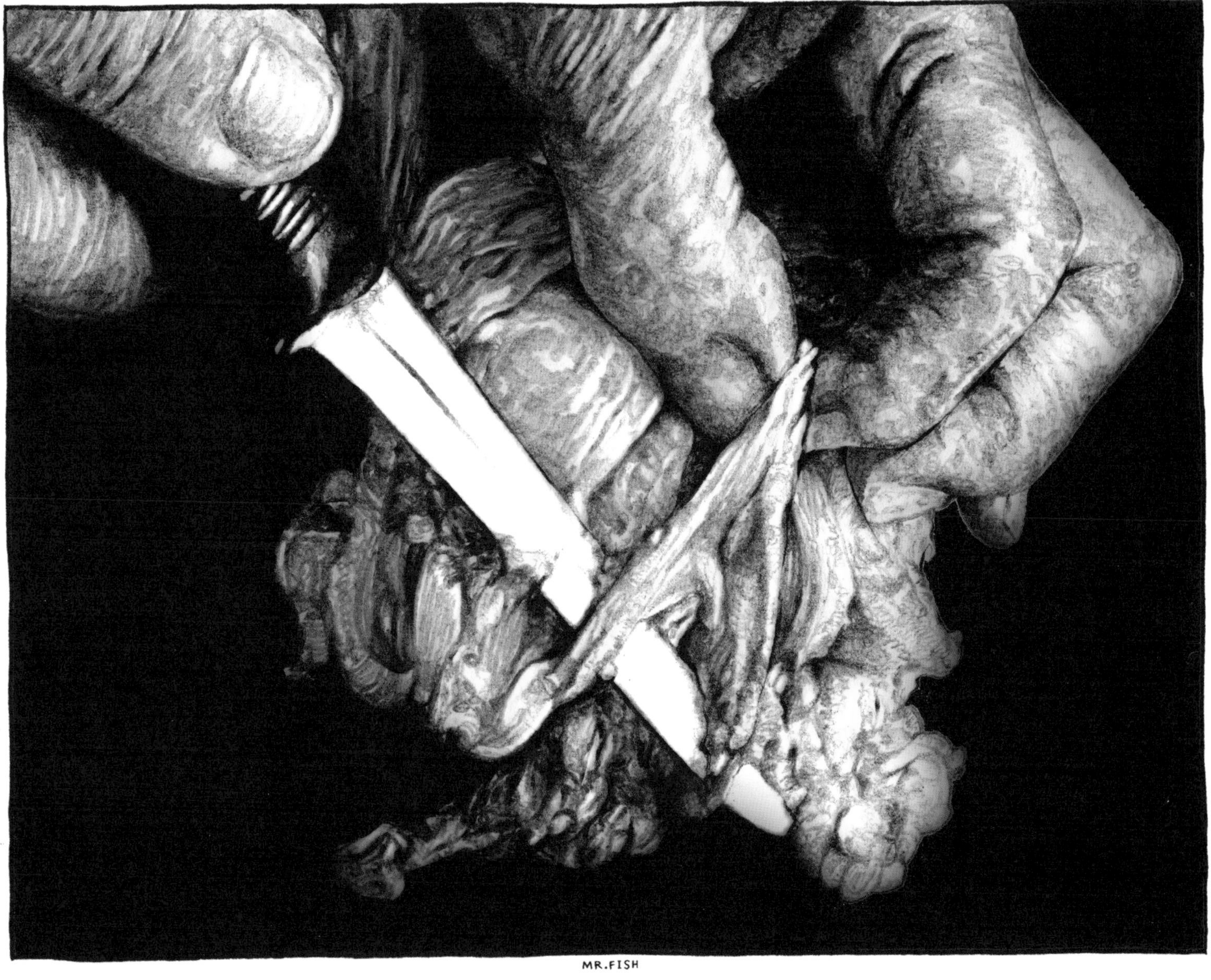

MR.FISH

I KNOW WHY THE CAGED BIRD SINGS
Maya Angelou

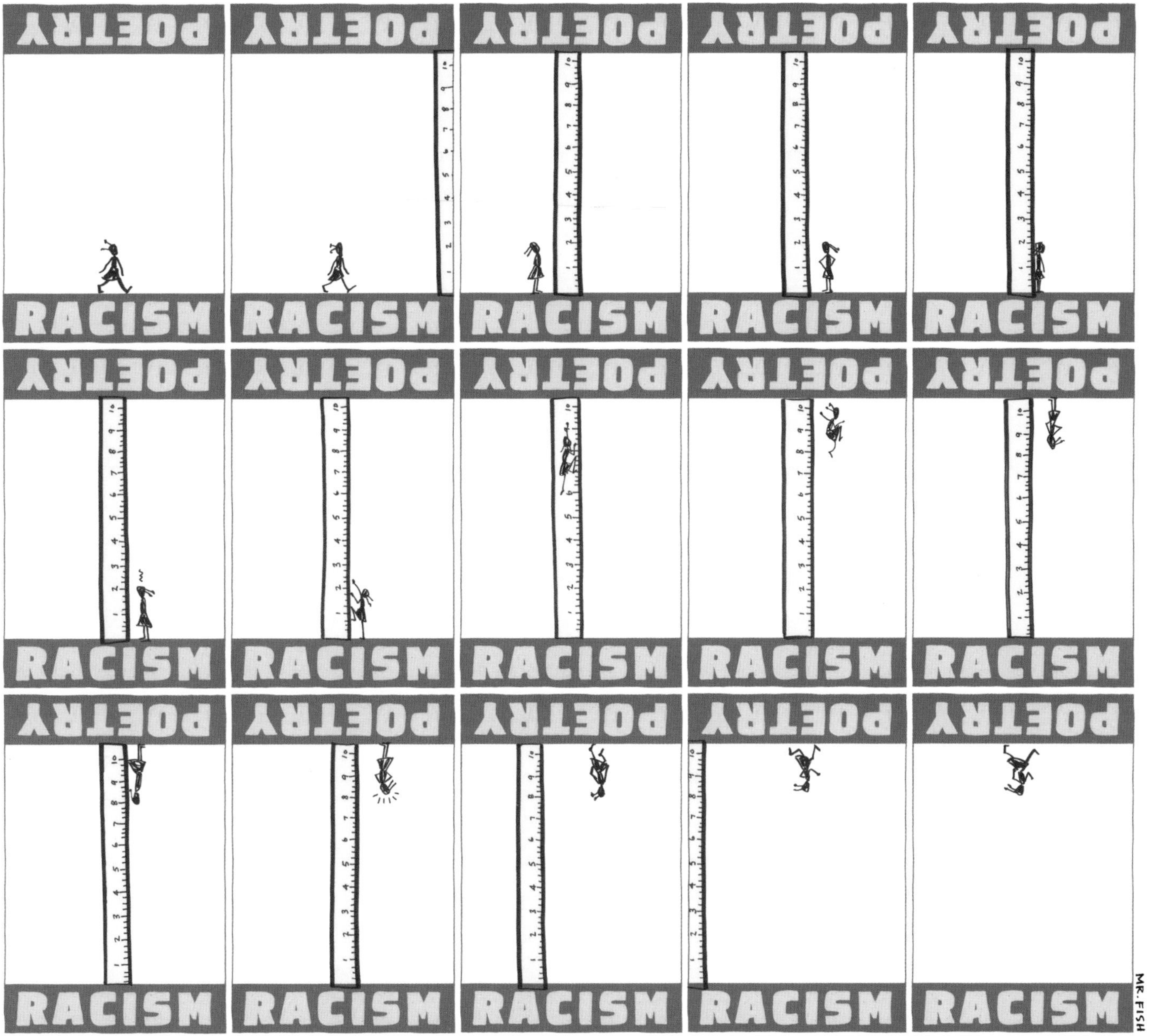
POETRY
RACISM
POETRY
RACISM
POETRY
RACISM
POETRY
RACISM
POETRY
RACISM
POETRY
RACISM
POETRY
RACISM
POETRY
RACISM
POETRY
RACISM
POETRY
RACISM
POETRY
RACISM
POETRY
RACISM
POETRY
RACISM
POETRY
RACISM
POETRY
RACISM
MR. FISH

NOTES FROM UNDERGROUND

Fyodor Dostoyevsky

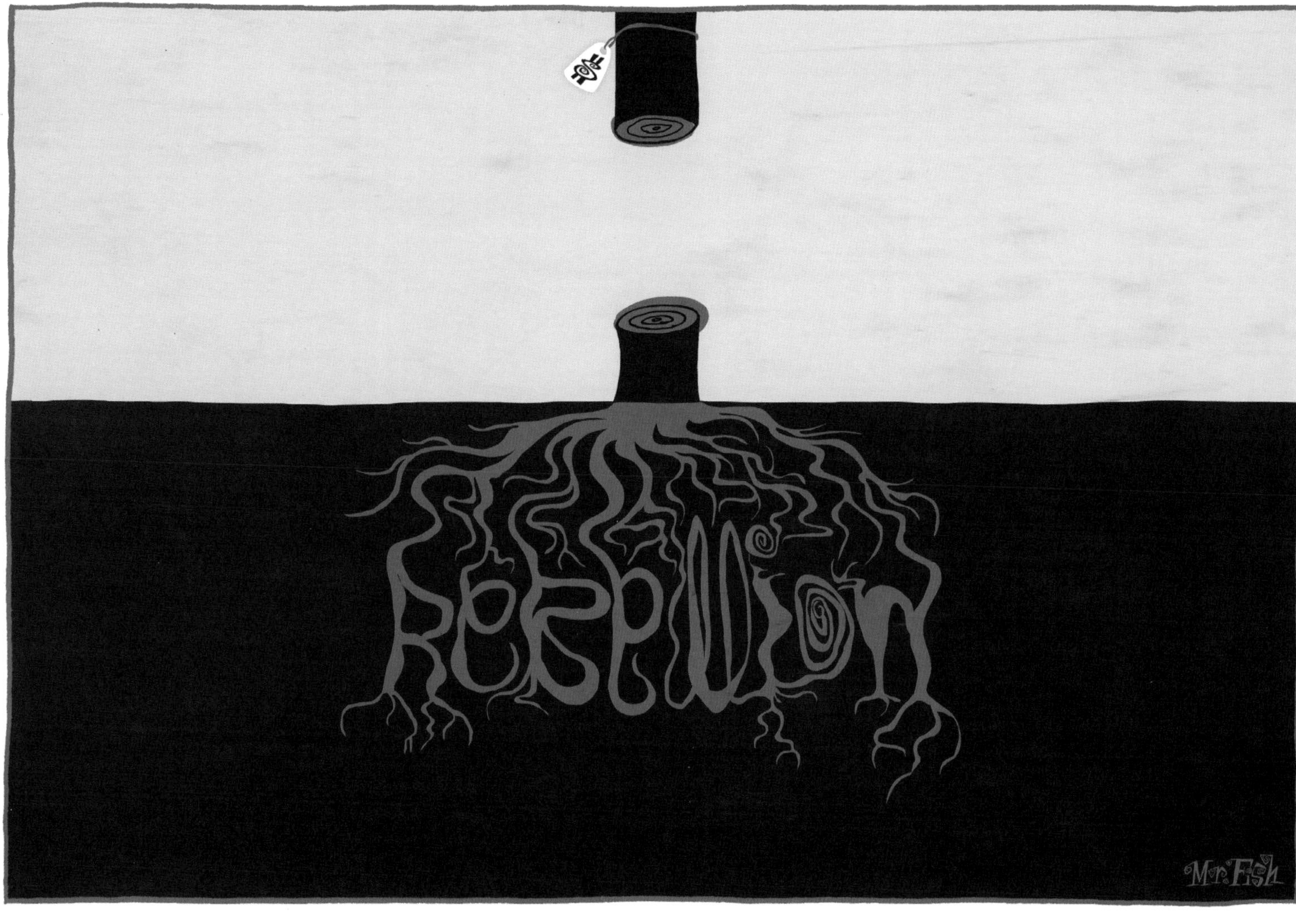
Rebellion
Mr. Fish

THE DIARY OF A YOUNG GIRL
Anne Frank

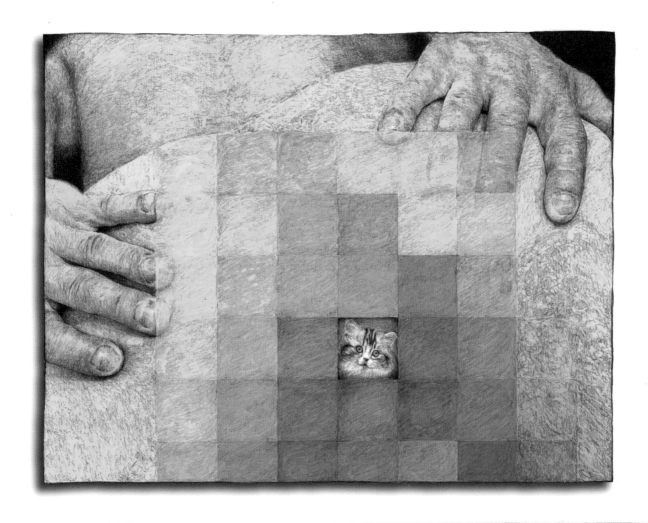

MR.FISH

THE LORD OF THE RINGS

J. R. R. Tolkien

ILLUSTRATION BY J. P. TROSTLE

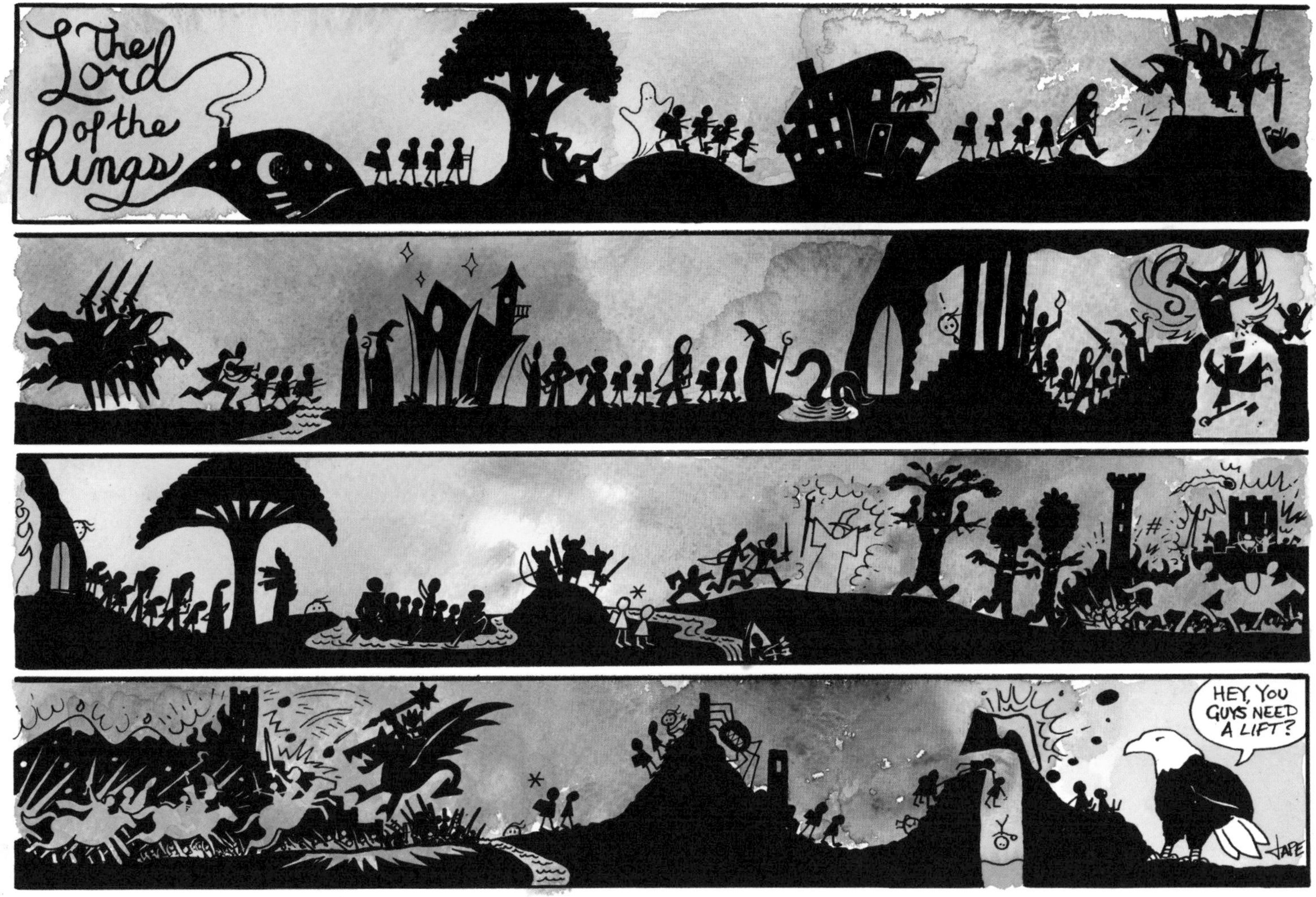
The Lord of the Rings
HEY, YOU GUYS NEED A LIFT?
JAPE

ON NARCISSISM
Sigmund Freud

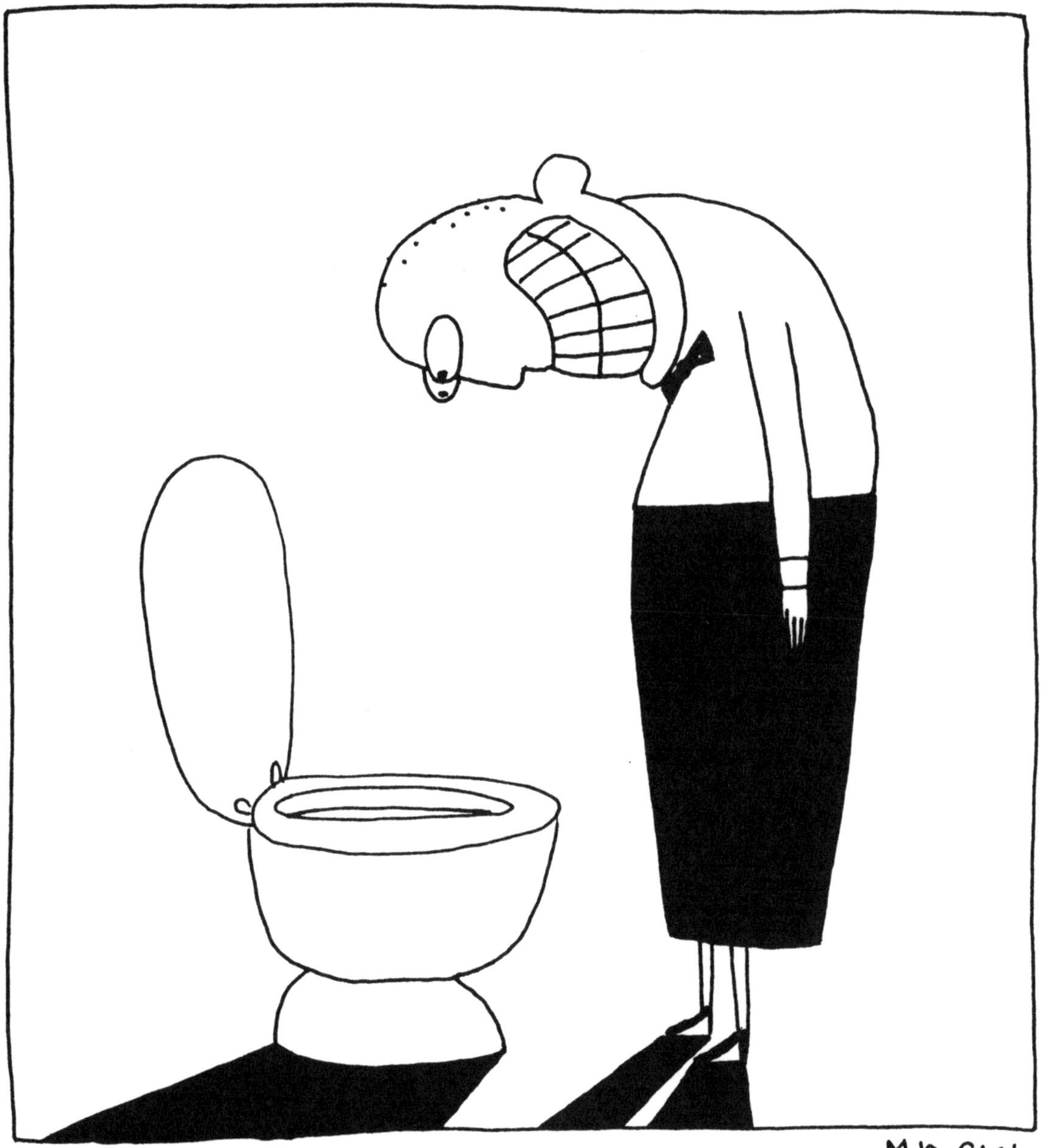

Mr. fish

A ROOM OF ONE'S OWN
Virginia Woolf

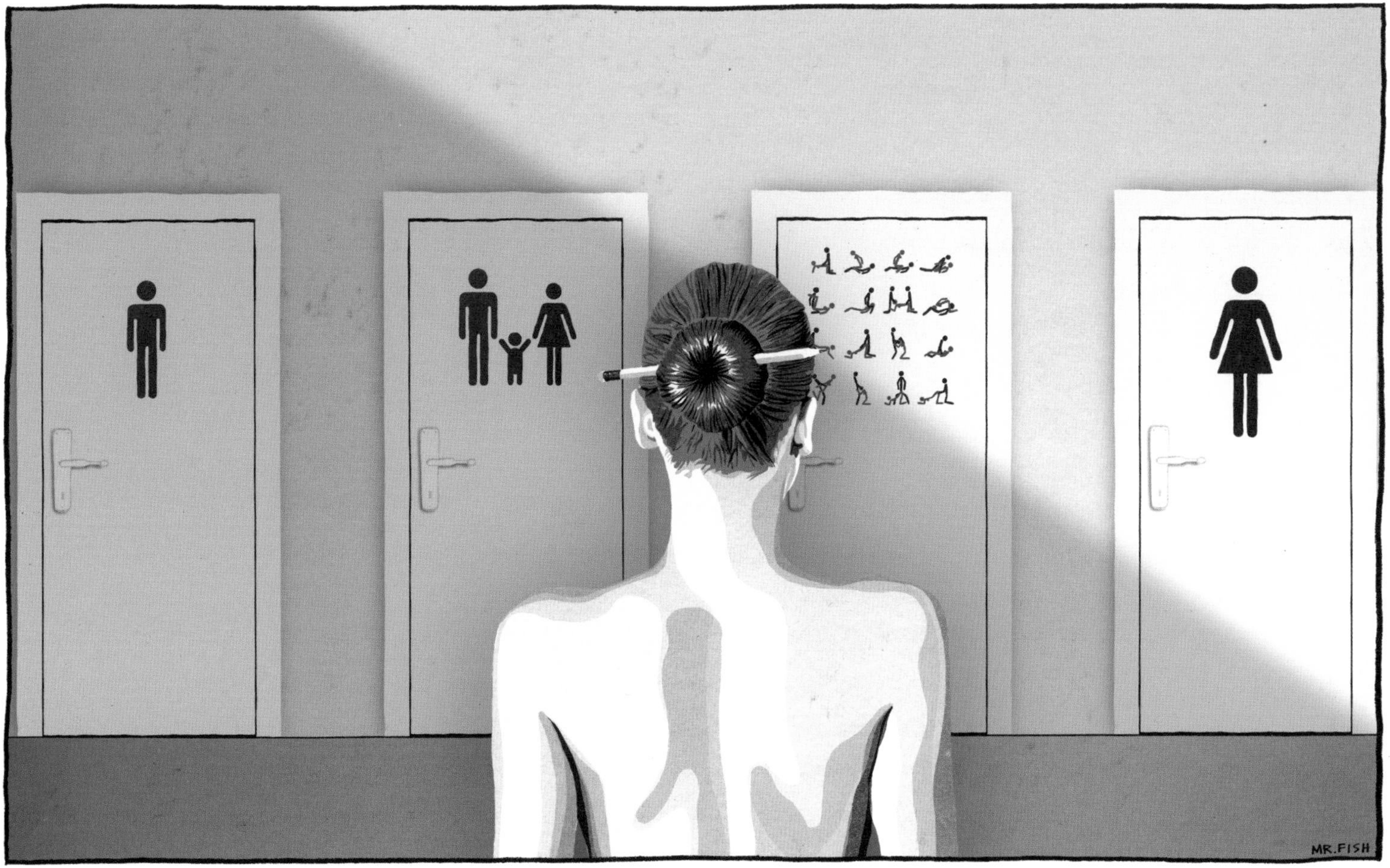
MR. FISH

THE WAR PRAYER

Mark Twain

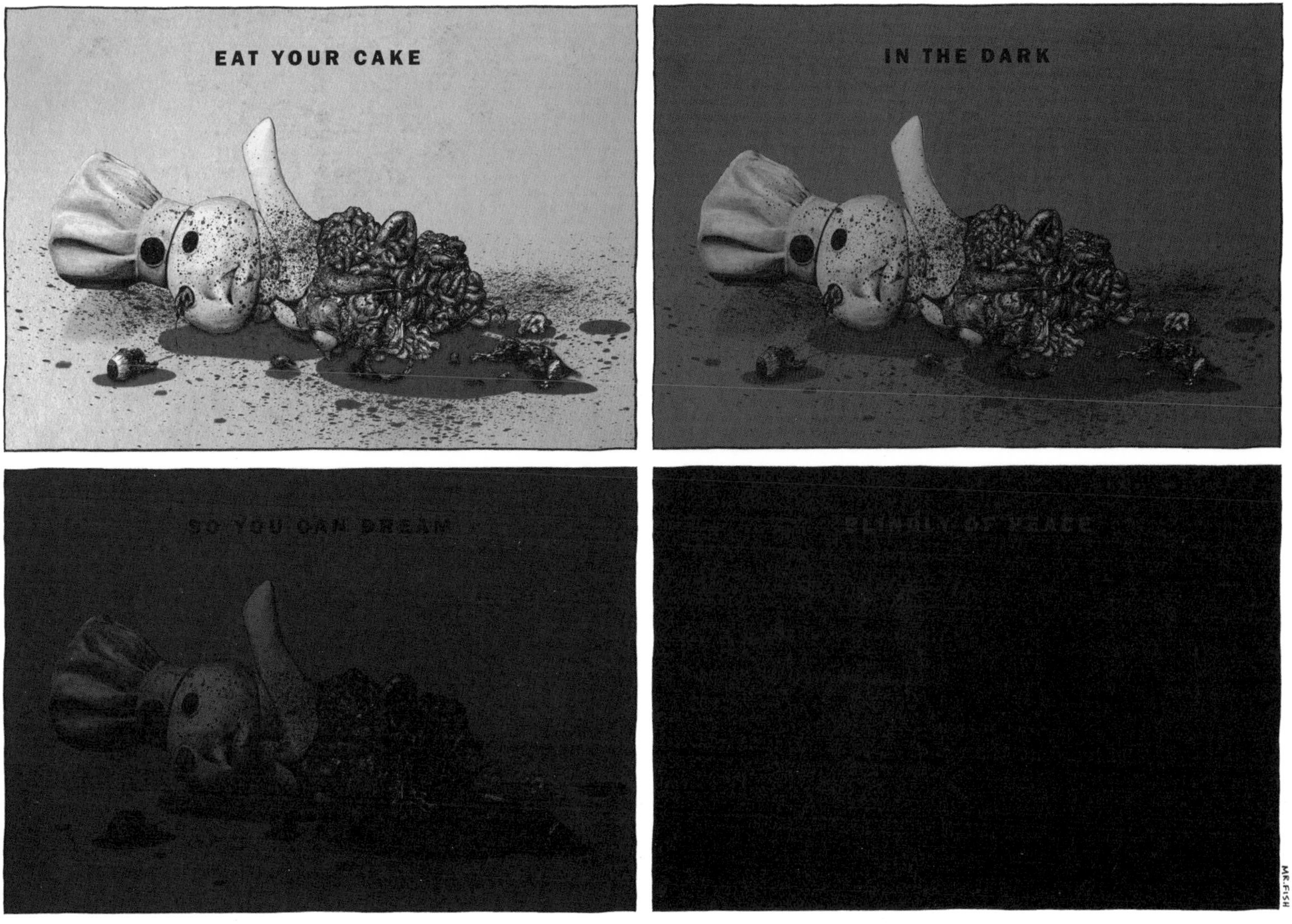
EAT YOUR CAKE
IN THE DARK
SO YOU CAN DREAM
MR.FISH

ON THE ORIGIN OF SPECIES

Charles Darwin

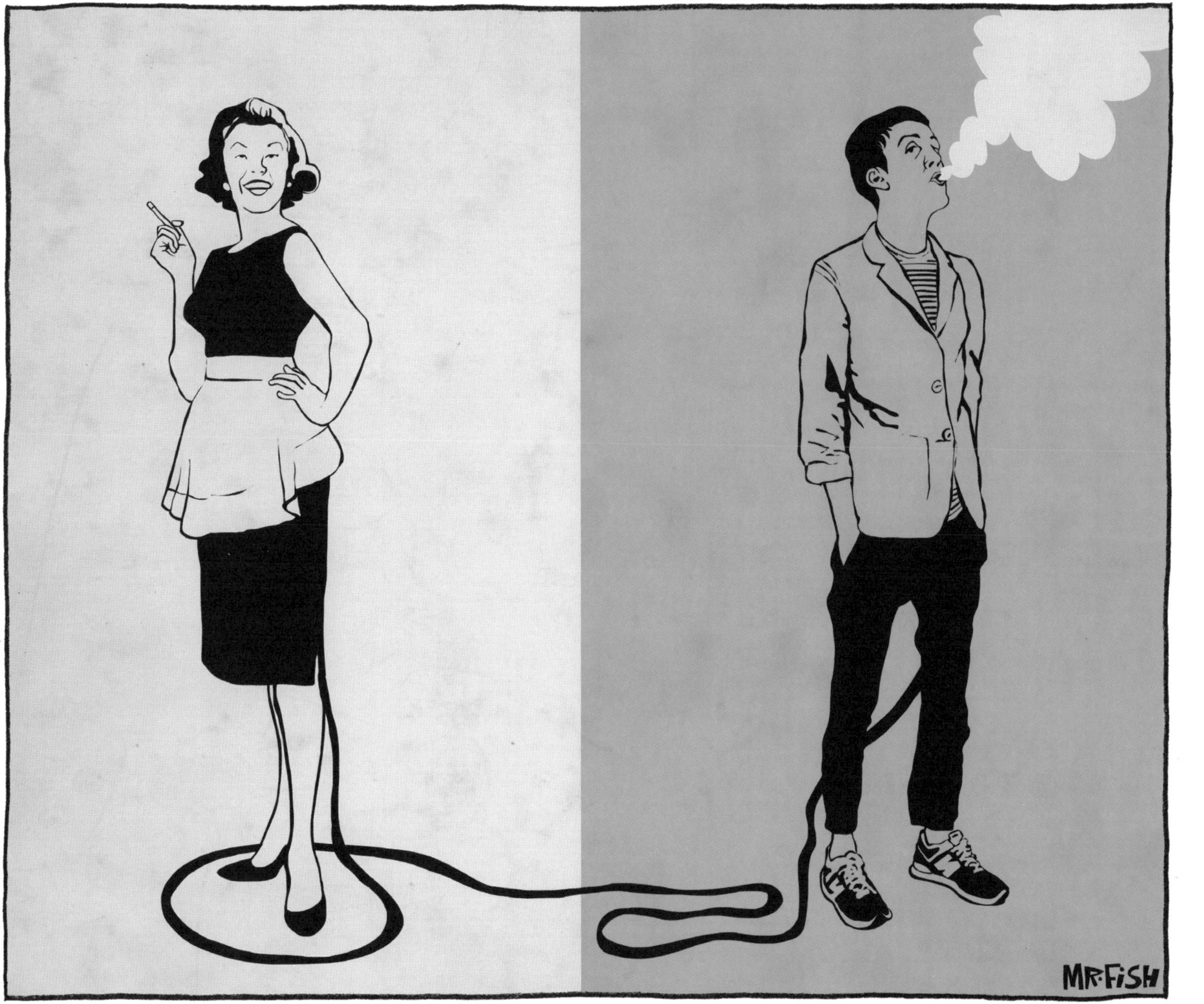
MR.FISH

THE INVISIBLE MAN

H. G. Wells

ILLUSTRATION BY JOHN KOVALESKI

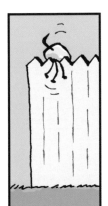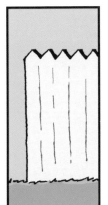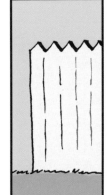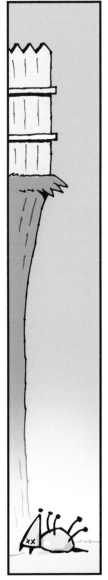

Kovaleski

AMERICAN PSYCHO

Bret Easton Ellis

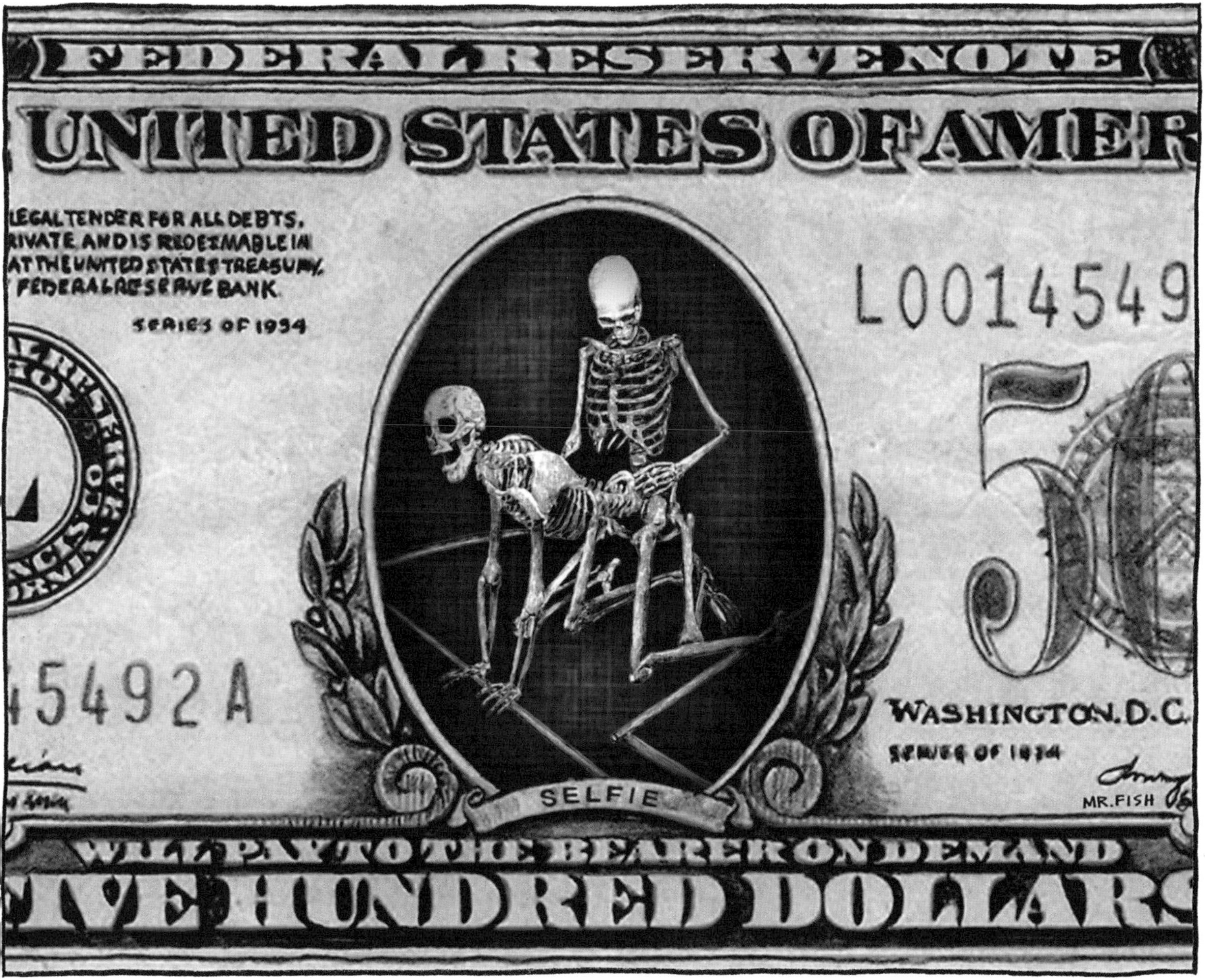
FEDERAL RESERVE NOTE
UNITED STATES OF AMER
LEGAL TENDER FOR ALL DEBTS,
RIVATE AND IS REDEEMABLE IN
AT THE UNITED STATES TREASURY,
FEDERAL RESERVE BANK
SERIES OF 1934
L0014549
5492A
WASHINGTON, D.C.
SELFIE
MR.FISH
WILL PAY TO THE BEARER ON DEMAND
IVE HUNDRED DOLLARS

WHY I AM NOT A CHRISTIAN

Bertrand Russell

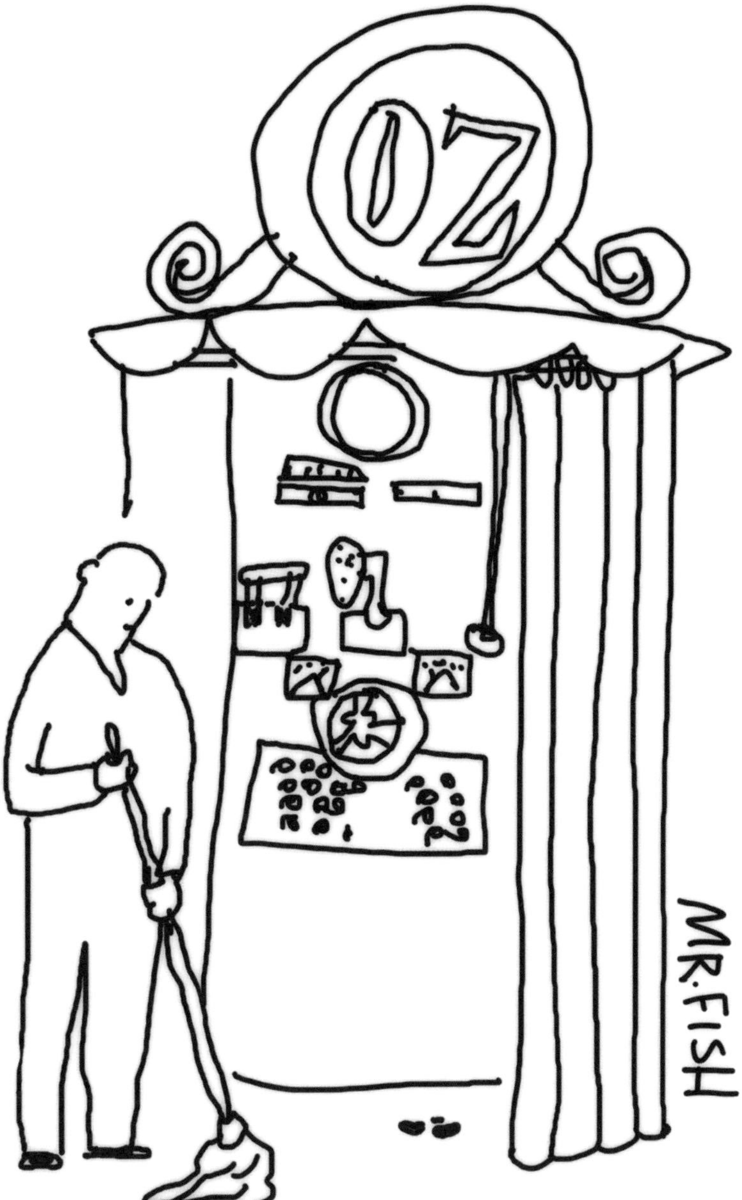
OZ
MR.FISH

ON THE ROAD
Jack Kerouac

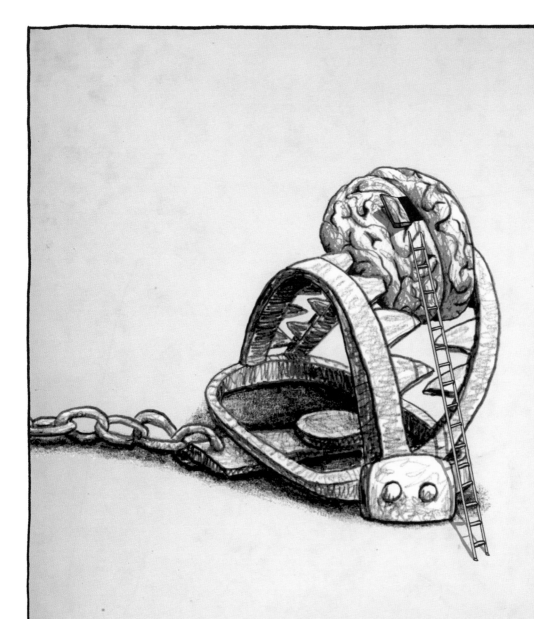

MR.FISH

FEAR OF FLYING

Erica Jong

ILLUSTRATION BY BETH McCASKEY

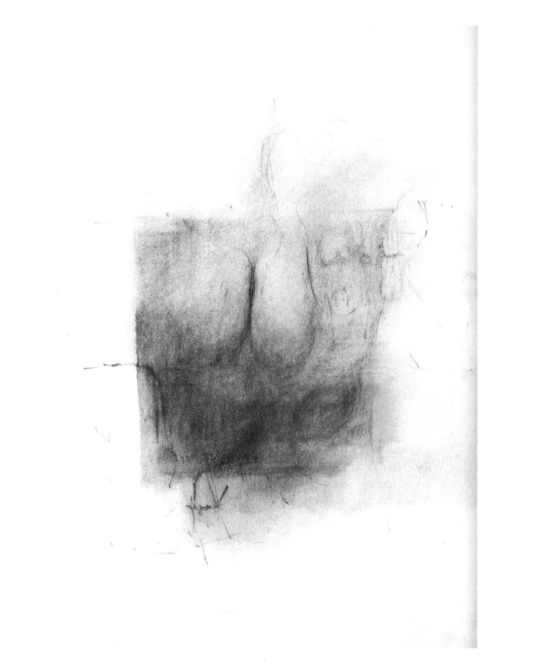

WIKIPEDIA

Everybody

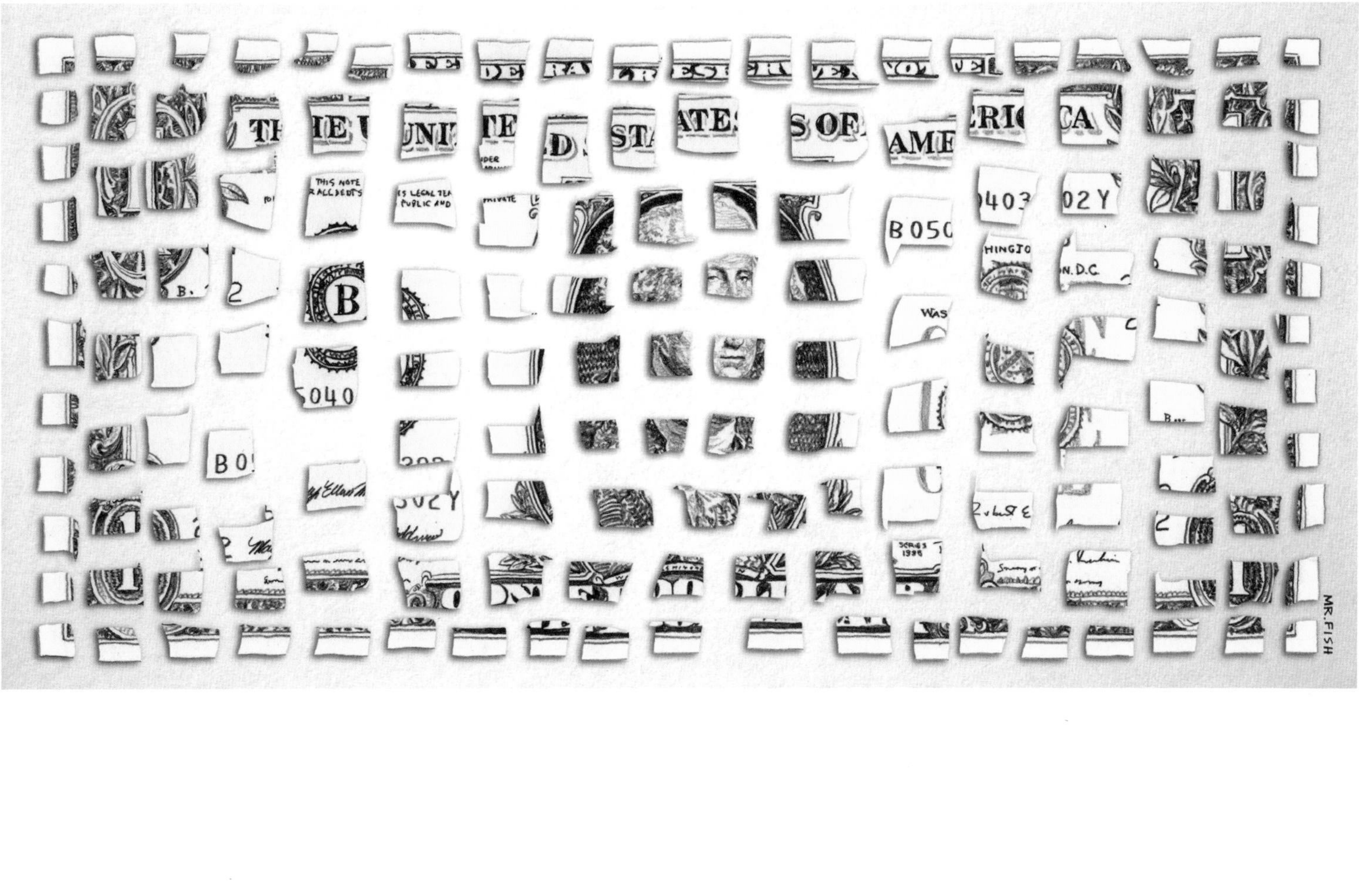
MR.FISH

WAR AND PEACE

Leo Tolstoy

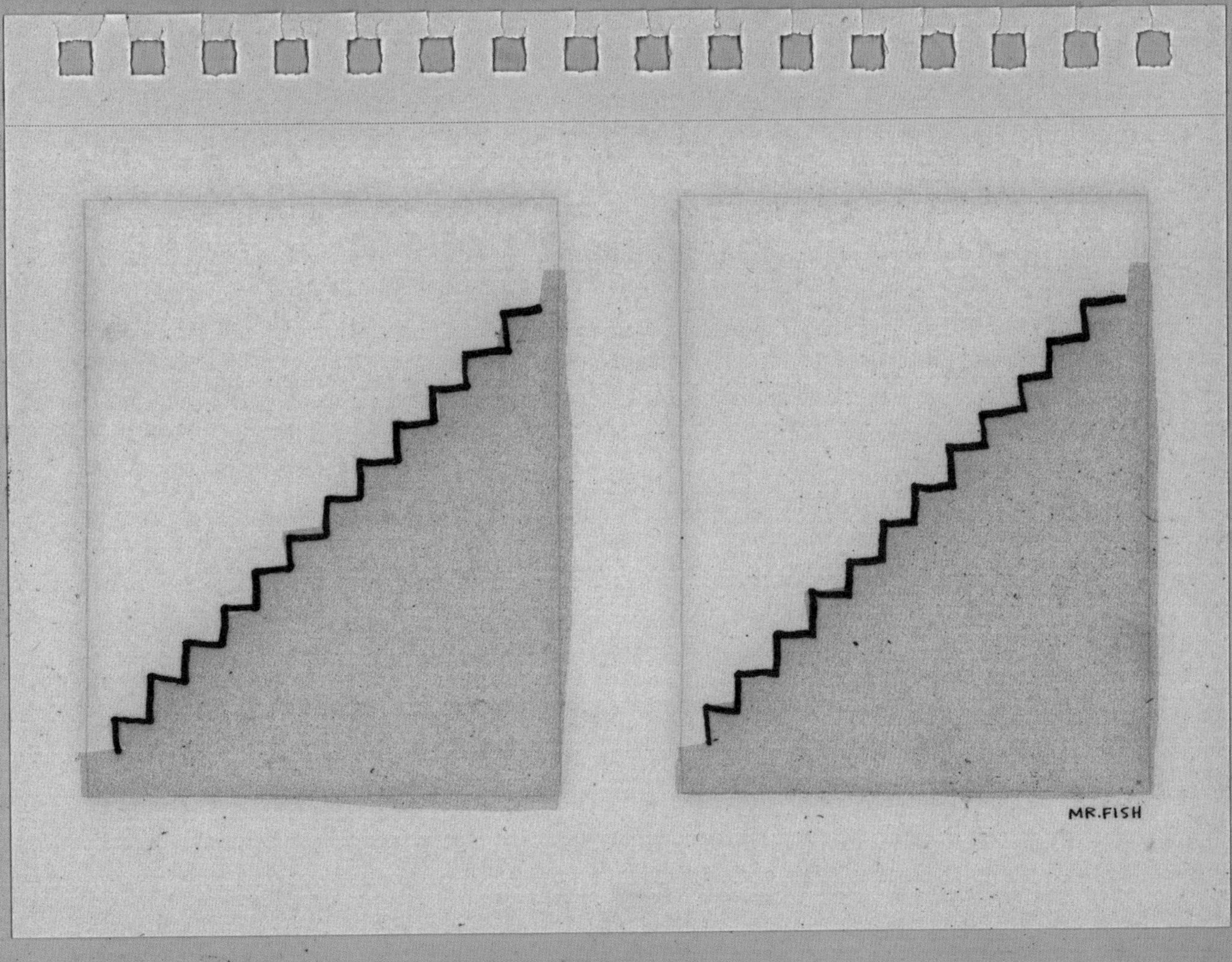
MR.FISH

ABOUT THE CONTRIBUTORS

SARAH AWAD received her BFA from Art Center College of Design and her MFA in painting from UCLA. Recent solo exhibitions include *Double Field* at Night Gallery and *Gate Paintings* at Diane Rosenstein Gallery, both in Los Angeles. Her paintings have been included in *Rogue Wave '13* at LA Louver Gallery and group exhibitions in Copenhagen, Vienna, New York, Seattle, Rotterdam, and Miami. She received the Joan Mitchell Foundation MFA grant in 2011 and her work has been reviewed in *Art in America, Modern Painter*, and *New American Painting*. She is a full-time faculty member at UC Irvine.

Somewhere in Brooklyn, **KEITH HENRY BROWN**'s mind wanders. A mainstream comics fan, he worked briefly at Marvel before beginning a career as an art director, working for such notable spots as Jazz at Lincoln Center and Blue Note, as well as many music labels. For Brown, music is one of the most essential things in life—that, and his two big sons. His personal comics tend to express the maladies of the everyday world, and he recently illustrated his first children's book, *Birth of the Cool: How Jazz Great Miles Davis Found His Sound*. For more information, visit www.keithhbrown.com.

Fredrik Bjerknes

SIRI DOKKEN has worked as an editorial cartoonist for the Oslo-based newspaper *Dagsavisen* since 1995. Apart from visual commentary on politics and society, she also does other projects, such as comics, book covers, and character design. Her drawings are regularly exhibited in Norway and abroad. For more information, visit www.siridokken.no.

MARISSA DOUGHERTY is an illustrative designer from New Jersey who creates in a broad range of styles for clients. She has a dual love for realism and simplistic design. Dougherty specializes in vector illustrations, branding, package design, hand lettering, and portrait design. Her love of monsters and the macabre influences her life, and she welcomes any opportunity to put a spooky twist on a project. In her free time, she can be found cooking damn good vegan food and drinking an old-fashioned. For more information, visit www.marissaskribbles.com.

Laura Dumm

GARY DUMM has loved comics since he was a kid and knows no other life than to make more of them. He collaborated with Harvey Pekar on his groundbreaking autobiographical *American Splendor* comic from its beginning in 1976, and has drawn graphic novels about life in America and American history with both Pekar and Paul Buhle. But his favorite collaborator is his wife Laura Dumm, on their current series of environmental paintings (with a political bent) that may be viewed on their website at www.dummart.org.

JOHN G. is an illustrator and comic creator who's been actively contributing to the Northeast Ohio arts and comics communities for nearly two decades. His published work includes the autobiographical comic *Tales to Demystify* and *Sandwich Anarchy: The Cult Culinary Posters of Melt Bar & Grilled*—an art book collecting his posters for grilled cheese sandwiches published by 1984 Publishing. He has collaborated with Jake Kelly on six issues of *The Lake Erie Monster*, a rust-belt horror anthology comic. He has also curated and edited *Cleveland Scene* magazine's annual comics issue since 2013. For more information, visit shinercomics.net.

ERIC J. GARCIA blends history, culture, contemporary themes, and a graphic style to create politically charged art that reaches beyond aesthetics. One of the few Chicano political satirists, Garcia has a unique perspective that offers new ways of visually and intellectually examining the United States. He is best known for his black-and-white, one-panel political cartoon series *El Machete Illustrated*. If you're looking for Sunday funnies look somewhere else, but if you want to pull down Uncle Sam's pants and see what's really going on, these are the cartoons for you. Garcia's caricatured critiques shred conservatives and disembowel liberals; wherever hypocrisy lurks the machete falls.

SAM HENDERSON has been in the field since graduating from the School of Visual Arts in 1992, working for Nickelodeon, *New York Press*, DC Comics, *Heavy Metal*, *Observer*, and many magazines. In 2002 he was nominated for an Emmy Award for his writing on *SpongeBob SquarePants*. He has had three collections of his work published, and after seemingly doing the same comic over and over for thirty years and it no longer sparking joy, he is working on a graphic memoir called *Hail Seizure*.

©Act3creative.com

RON HILL lives in his hometown of Cleveland, Ohio, and is a graduate of the Art Institute of Pittsburgh. He has been a designer, illustrator, caricaturist, educator, and cartoonist for forty years. As an illustrator, he has drawn for Dungeons & Dragons, Westminster John Knox Press, and the Cleveland Indians, to name just a few clients. A member of the American Association of Editorial Cartoonists, his latest cartoon collection was published by Act 3 in 2019; *The Usual Suspects* is a collection of his cartoons from twenty years with the award-winning *Chagrin Valley Times*, and available at act3creative.com.

Phil Hollman

TAMI KNIGHT is a western Canadian cartoonist who has been poking fun at mountaineering and climbers for forty years. Regularly published in *Alpinist Magazine*, she has seven books of cartoons extant including *Everest, the Ultimate Hump,* which, in addition to being short-listed for the Banff Mountain Book Festival literary prize, anticipated some of the present Everest insanity. Her work was included in the anthology *Waymaking.* She likes cider, chocolate, cats, zero tides, riding her scooter, and handstands in public places.

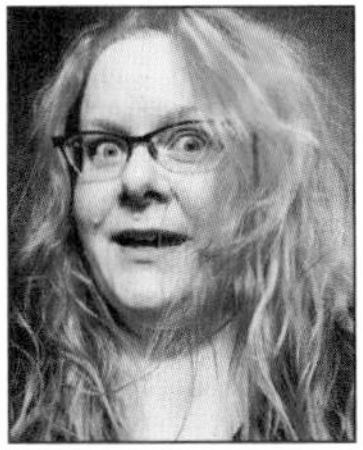

Bathroom selfie

TAMARA KNOSS, often proclaimed to be naive and delusional, is the darkest time-line version of Phoebe Caulfield. She has mastered the art of refusing to grow up by working as an artist in the video game industry since 2000. Knoss spends her days discerning loathsome truths, snuggling her puppy, and grabbing brass rings.

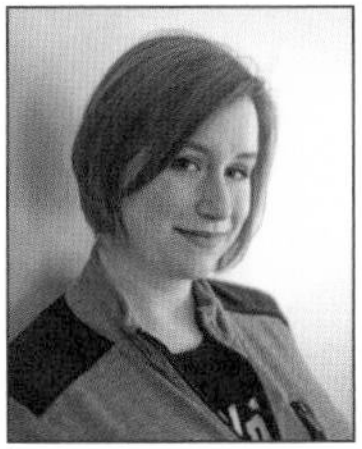

Tim Switalski

CLARE KOLAT is a contemporary surrealist artist, comic creator, and designer from Cleveland, Ohio. She has a flair for the fantastic, and her work often bursts with bold colors and cheeky winks to the viewer. The feminine and natural realm are common themes in her work as she juxtaposes her figures with flora and fauna in sensual, magical dreamscapes.

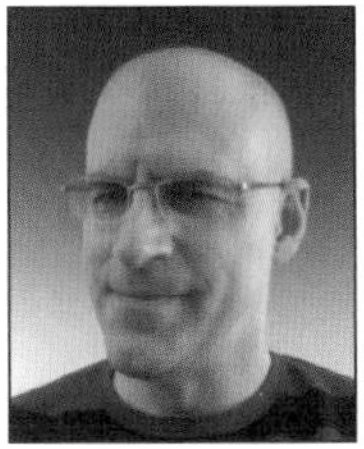

JOHN KOVALESKI is a cartoonist, writer, and teacher. In addition to being the creator of the comic strips *Daddy Daze* and *Bo Nanas*, he has also been a contributor to *MAD Magazine*, illustrated credit sequences for motion pictures, and created animated greeting cards for Amazon.com.

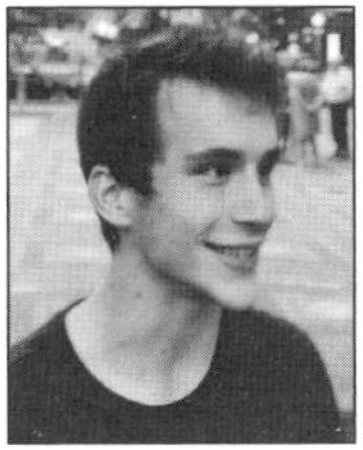

LODI MARASESCU is a self-taught French amateur cartoonist and is currently pursuing studies in French literature. He contributes to a student newspaper in Paris and is willing to tackle others. Cafés are his workshops, where he's trying to develop his character Blaise, a simple guy. He's influenced by satirical cartoons as much as graphic and abstract work, provoking a vintage old-fashioned style. His work is based on the principle of simplicity and variation.

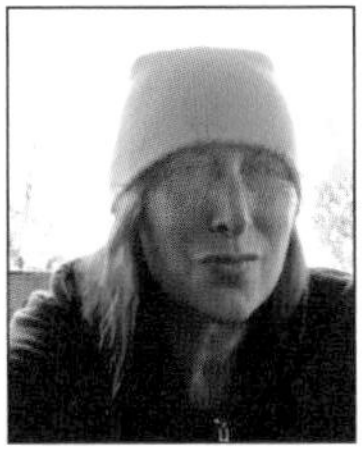

Bettina Uoma

BETH McCASKEY lives in Pennsylvania. She likes riding bicycles and does *not* have a fear of flying.

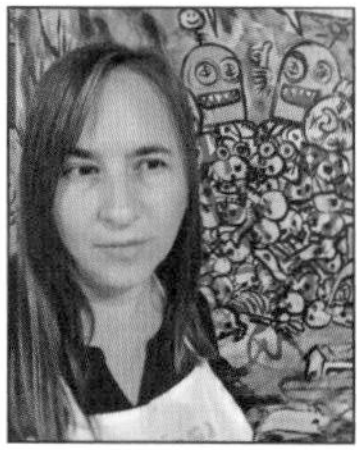

STEPHANIE McMILLAN's award-winning comics, editorial cartoons, and illustrations have appeared worldwide in hundreds of print and online publications, plus numerous textbooks and grassroots protest leaflets. She is the creator of the perpetual desk calendar "365 Daily Affirmations for Revolutionary Proletarian Militants" and the author of several books including *Capitalism Must Die!* Currently she creates artwork in various media, with commentary, advocating global, working class–led revolution. For more information, visit stephaniemcmillan.org; or find her on Instagram: @steph.mcmillan.

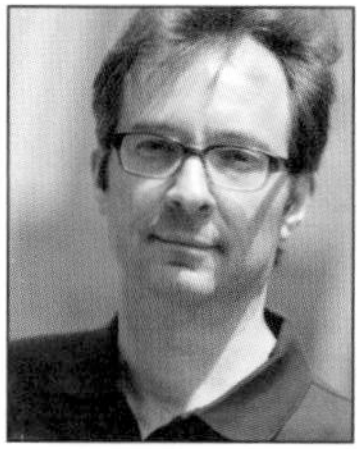

TED RALL bridges the gap between edgy countercultural cartooning on the left and mainstream visibility in corporate media. Syndicated in nearly a hundred newspapers, Rall is a Pulitzer Prize finalist, author of twenty books, graphic novelist, and occasional conflict reporter. His notable titles include the Gen X manifesto *Revenge of the Latchkey Kids*, the graphic travelogue *To Afghanistan and Back,* and the *New York Times* best sellers *Bernie* and *Snowden*. For more information, visit rall.com.

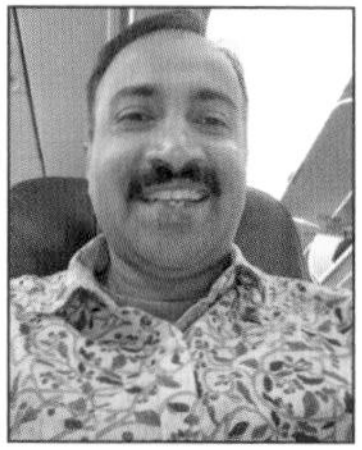

SURAG RAMACHANDRAN is an award-winning cartoonist and author from India. He is working as assistant vice president and head of product content and learning at MBB Labs, the global innovation center of Maybank. Ramachandran is more of a writer who can draw than an artist who can write. His unique mix of art, words, and technical skills has enabled him to come up with cartoon explainer videos in his corporate career. He has written extensively for both children and adult readers. His drawings are digitally developed and are used either independently or to enhance his stories.

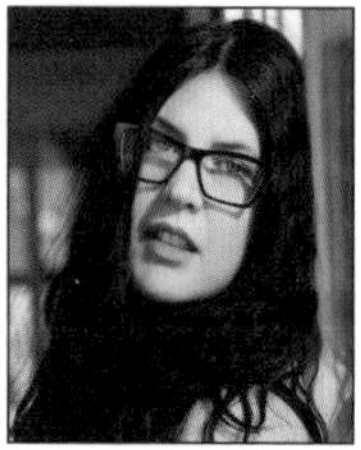

NathalieRosePhotography.com

TARA SEIBEL is best known for her collaboration with the late Harvey Pekar of *American Splendor* comics. She worked at American Greetings and spearheaded the Tara Seibel Art Gallery in Cleveland. Her editorial cartoons and graphic stories have been published in *The Graphic Canon* volumes 2 and 3, *The Graphic Canon of Children's Literature, Comic's Comics, Mineshaft, Jewish Review of Books, New York Times, Los Angeles Times, Cleveland Scene, Austin Chronicle, Heeb, Hippy Comix,* and *USA Today*'s Pop Candy. She teaches at Fairmount Center for the Arts. Seibel lives with her husband Aaron, three children, a dog, and a cat in Pepper Pike, Ohio. For more information, visit taraseibelart.com.

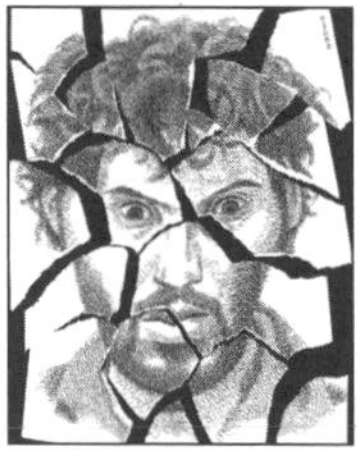

ANDY SINGER has drawn cartoons and illustrations for over twenty-five years. His work appears mostly in the alternative press but occasionally in more mainstream venues. He's the author of four books. His first book, *CARtoons* (2001), has been translated into five languages. Despite this, he barely makes minimum wage and mostly lives off his wife's excellent teaching salary. So if you're an editor or publisher and have work to offer, FOR GOD's SAKE, CALL ANDY IMMEDIATELY! You can see more of his work at www.andysinger.com.

BENJAMIN SLYNGSTAD is a cartoonist and illustrator born in Los Angeles, California. His work has been featured in publications such as the *Sentinel* newspaper and *Written By* magazine. Slyngstad is often recognized for his ability to address complex issues in a clear and concise visual fashion.

J. P. TROSTLE (a.k.a. Jape) is an illustrator and political artist based in Durham, North Carolina. A long-time veteran of the newspaper industry, he worked as an editorial cartoonist and graphic designer for several dailies and an alt-weekly—until he suddenly didn't. He's been art director and editor for half a dozen books on political cartooning, including the three-volume *Attitude* series with cartoonist Ted Rall. Trostle has received an odd assortment of awards, including first place in illustration in 2013 from the Association of Alternative Newsmedia. He is currently online editor for the Association of American Editorial Cartoonists.

Marc Crabtree

WES TYRELL is a one-time country music crooner and fencing enthusiast who enjoys the challenge of cartooning "Prophet of Zoom" for *Zoomer* magazine in Canada. From his Toronto studio, Tyrell has been producing humorous editorial cartoons and illustrations for over twenty years. President of the Association of Canadian Cartoonists since 2012, he has the honor of representing colleagues who draw for the nation's newspapers and magazines. In 2019 he published a cartoon book on the sexual habits of Canadians that is bound to amuse and alarm—*Sex in a Snowbank*.

NATE ULSH is a Brooklyn-based musician, visual artist, audiophile, and food nerd who splits his time between drooling over vinyl and vintage guitars and writing music for his psychedelic pop outfit, Toebow. Whether it's drawing abstract contour lines, weaving melodic guitar loops, or creating some version of sautéed kale, his inspiration is always fast and dirty. A self-proclaimed "idea blurter," Ulsh revels in the moment, savoring the feeling of creating rather than the drudgery of premeditated concepts. When he's not tinkering with his hi-fi sound system or writing on the guitar, his days are mostly spent in the kitchen cooking with his girlfriend Emily and juggling seven kittens.

Loubna Mrie

ELI VALLEY is a writer and artist whose work has been featured in the *Nation*, the *New Republic*, the *Nib*, the *Daily Beast, Gawker, The Best American Comics*, and elsewhere. His art has been labeled "ferociously repugnant" by *Commentary* and "hilarious" by the *Comics Journal*. His book *Diaspora Boy: Comics on Crisis in America and Israel* was heralded as "one of the most fascinating and darkly humorous books in living memory" by the *Los Angeles Review of Books*, and his art is featured in *The Chapo Guide to Revolution: A Manifesto Against Logic, Facts, and Reason*. His website is www.elivalley.com.

ABOUT MR. FISH

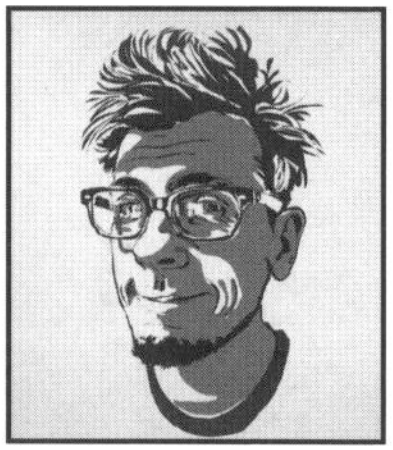

MR. FISH lives in Philadelphia, Pennsylvania. Occasionally, he laughs his head off. His mother has no idea what he's up to. She cries easily. For more information, date him.

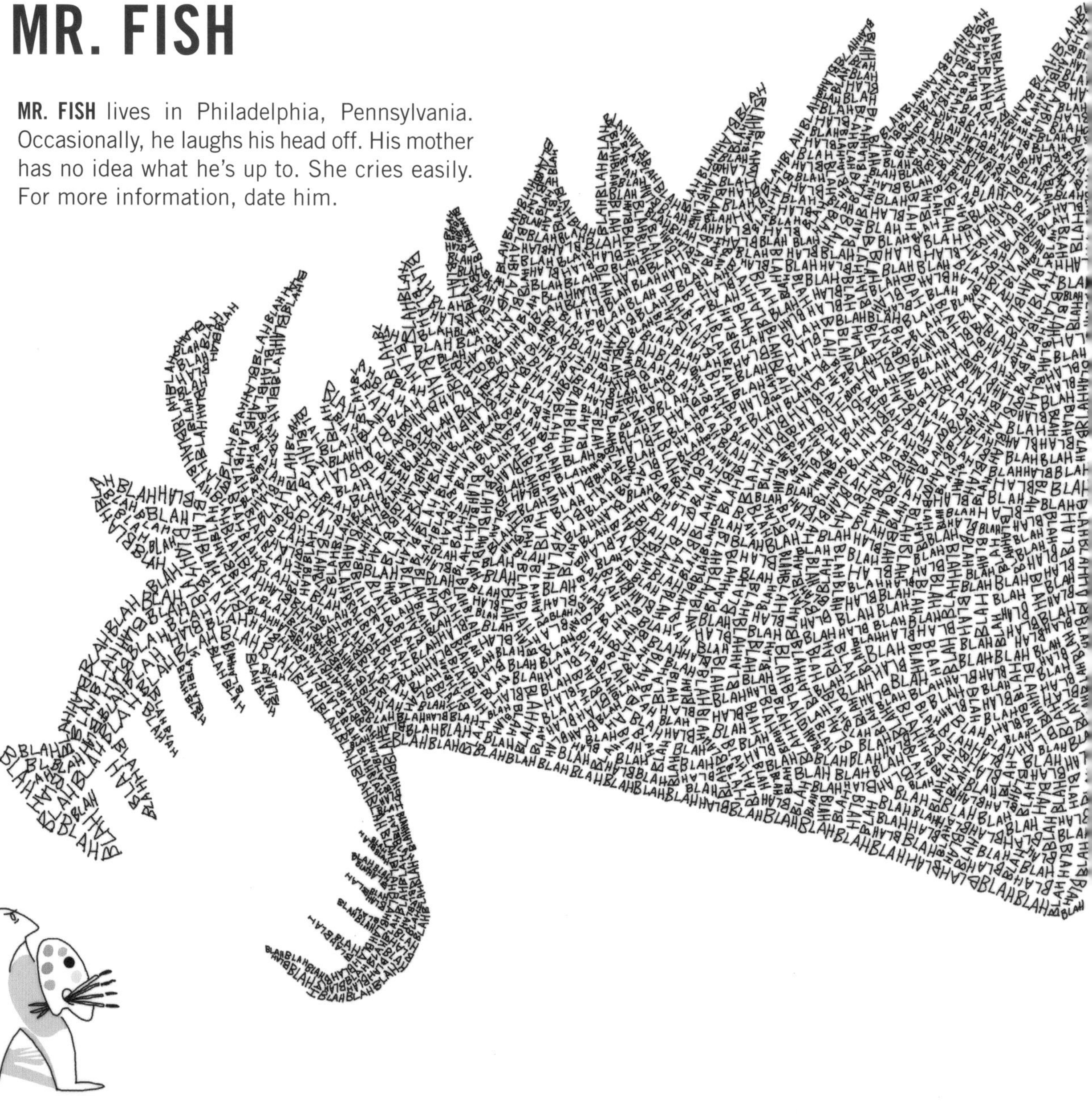